KEEPING
IT ON
THE ROAD

KEEPING IT ON THE ROAD

How to Buy a Car You'll Love,
Help It Live over 100,000 Miles,
and Smile When You Kiss It Good-bye

WYNN MOORE

QUILL

New York   1982

Library of Congress Cataloging in Publication Data

Moore, Wynn.
  Keeping it on the road.

  Includes index.
  1. Automobiles—Purchasing.   2. Automobiles—Maintenance and repair.   I. Title.
[TL162.M64]   629.2′222   81-22754
ISBN 0-688-01013-X (pbk.)   AACR2

Printed in the United States of America

First Quill Edition

1 2 3 4 5 6 7 8 9 10

CONTENTS

The Do-It-Yourself Manual for People Who Never Do Anything Themselves

Fill It Up and Check the Oil

Good-bye, Old Friend—We Complete the 100,000-Mile Circle

ANOTHER DO-IT-YOURSELF BOOK? WHO NEEDS IT?

In today's world, people seem to make all their choices the same way. Whether it's a mate, a suit of clothes, a religion, or an automobile, usually you can bet on their choice of any one area by their choice in the others. Some want flash and trappings with everything automatic and easy. Others want just the basics, the stripped-down model that does the job without ostentation. Unfortunately, though, everyone does not make the right choice, and even when he or she does, all choices need tender, loving care and attention to get the most out of them.

Statistics tell us that one out of every three marriages and one out of every three cars ends up on the junk heap in the first five years. My humanitarian instincts tell me I must do something about this. I have decided to try to save you some money and aggravation with your car.

Certain rules and attention to simple basics can keep your car off the junk heap. There is no reason why any car, regardless of where it is produced, cannot go at least 100,000 miles, and most should go twice that distance. It makes no difference if the car was produced by elves in the Black Forest, Oriental magicians, or union devils from the urban jungles of Detroit—the end product will last only as long as you, the buyer, take care of it and give it tender love and the proper weight oil. This book will attempt to take you from the day when you think of buying a car right through to the last day you own it, and with luck and proper care, many years down the line.

No one expects you to be able to do all the repairs yourself—but certain items *anybody* can manage, and knowing what the problem is can save you from the greedy or ignorant repair-shop employee. We will start by trying to save you some money when you buy your new car, move on to helping you make your car last longer than you thought possible, and close the circle with tips on selling your old car.

Being an underprivileged child, I did not get my first car until I was 18. (I must have been underprivileged, because my four sons all insist that everybody has a car as soon as he or she turns 16.) Yet being a true-blue American, I was in love with cars long before I found out about the opposite sex, and the September new-car showings at the local dealers were worth a lot more time than the Miss America contest that took place 60 miles away at Atlantic City. In fact, I know of no teenager in my Philadelphia neighborhood who ever traveled to the Miss America Pageant, but none ever missed the first day of showings at the Broad Street car dealers a few blocks away.

My first car, bought in 1952, was a four-year-old Hudson Straight Eight. I bought it shortly after getting my first paying job as a radio announcer in Philadelphia. Both the car and the radio-station equipment responded in the same way. When they stopped, you fixed them with a string of curses and a few well-placed kicks. The Hudson died 3 years later in West Virginia, and I decided I needed to buy better cars or learn more about the other ones. Economics made the latter course necessary, and since then I have done most of my own car repairs, prepared and raced my own sports cars, and owned three separate collections of classic and antique cars, and am now working on my fourth car collection.

By the way, of the 13 cars I now own, 5 have over 100,000 miles on them. They are all used regularly, and I would trust any one of them to take me across the country in any weather and at any time of year.

Is Now the Time to Buy One?

Through the 1980s, people will be stumped by too many changes, too fast, in the world of automobiles and in transportation in general. The government keeps talking about mass transportation, but Fred and Harriet in the suburbs cannot find a taxi when they need one, let alone take a bus or train to the shopping center or to work.

The cities have spewed people out to the lush life of the suburbs over the past 30 years, and suddenly the only lush thing in the neighborhood is the guy three doors down who dropped out of Alcoholics Anonymous. Getting anywhere on most transit systems requires a crystal ball for the timetable and a suit of armor. Subways have become public urinals, and buses huge rolling billboards for graffiti artists.

As much as the feds talk about mass transit, their own reports indicate that for the next 20 years or more, the car is going to be the main means of transportation in this country. Blame it on oil-company lobbying, highway trust-fund pork-barreling, auto-company advertising, or what have you, the United States has become an automobile economy in the past three decades, and that will not change overnight. Thirty years of road building in place of mass-transit development will not be transformed by magic into new rail lines and bus routes. The oil shortage notwithstanding, the United States is a nation trapped into its automobiles, and it will not break out of that bind fast enough to make any difference to you if you expect to need another car soon.

The question is, buy it now or buy it later?

The Wave of the Future

If Fred down the street tells you he heard that there will be a great breakthrough in gas mileage in the cars coming out in 2 or 3 years, tell him the only breakthrough will be the installation of pedals and a chain for those who want to use muscle power in place of gasoline. The fact of the matter is that Detroit and the other auto centers of the world are stuck with only one real option for the next 10 to 15 years. The cars will be getting smaller, the engines will be getting smaller, and the use of more plastics will make even the small cars lighter. Research is going on to make more efficient engines for automobiles and trucks, but don't expect much in the near future. Mandrake the Magician is not in the car business, and the facts of life say that the companies must get as much use as possible out of what they have before they spend billions of dollars to switch over to new power sources, if they do find them. To give you an idea of what this means, look at the very few companies trying to sell electric cars today. Most are using Detroit-built cars with the guts replaced by electric motors and batteries. One company claims to have designed a new electric car from the ground up. You can buy this marvel for only $25,000 a copy. It seats four and will go 60 to 75 miles on one charge. It is doubtful that there will be a path beaten to the manufacturer's door.

Nonetheless electric cars *are* in the future. No less a personage than the top executive at General Motors has said that by 1995 half of the cars built in this country will be electric. He expects 1990 to be the first year of significant electric-car sales. The first GM electric car will be on the market by 1985.

Remember this: As long as the giants of the industry are doing their planning for ten years down the road, you can expect that they know what they are doing. Small companies looking to jump into the void created by the lack of a mass-produced electric car will be forced to charge high prices for cars that will not meet American drivers' needs, because they just do not have the financing or facilities to build cars in the necessary mass-production numbers to bring the price down. The market for a mass-produced electric car is just not there when these cars can go only 50 or 75 miles without being recharged for 8 hours. If a battery breakthrough that will allow 150-mile trips or more occurs, these cars will begin to sell.

The battery companies are working double time to come up with such a breakthrough, but so far it does not look as if one will happen in the near future.

The government says that most of the innovations in cars will come in two waves, one immediately and the second by the end of the 1990s. You are seeing the first wave—the downsizing of the cars, the move to front-wheel drive, the use of more and more plastic in all models, and such things as computerized sensing devices to meter fuel supply along with new automatic transmissions that go into overdrive on the road or lock up in high gear to prevent slippage. All of these innovations are here now. Again, there may be improvements in the next 5 years but, basically, the cars you see today will be much the same as those you see in 1985—that is, the smaller ones. You can expect that the large car 5 years from now will be the size of today's compact car. You may also see some of the minicars that run around the streets of Japan and Germany. They are smaller than the smallest Honda, Colt, or Le Car now available.

The Future Is Now

What all this means is that you can actually buy a car today that will still be close to the state of the art 5 years from today. If this bursts your balloon because you thought you were smart to wait, I can only say that if you waited this long, you have suffered enough. The real revolution in cars has been going on for the last 5 years, and for the next 5 years automobile companies will be refining the advances they have already made. The changes from here on will be minor in general because by 1985 the companies will have spent over $50 billion in order to meet federal pollution laws, federal crash-resistance laws, and federal gas-mileage demands. Along with the federal regulations that have to be met, the manufacturers are faced with a public that has been watching gas prices soar past the $1.50 mark. They have been scared out of big comfortable bathtubs and are demanding portable washbasins.

Detroit is doing everything it can to make believe they have conquered the mileage problem. They are touting 4-cylinder and 6-cylinder cars and trying to make the public believe that the number of cylinders makes a difference in mileage. The fact is that the displacement of the cylinders and the horsepower available in those cylinders are the real answer, and 4-cylinder engines large enough to move big cars will get the same mileage as the same size eight. Sound confusing? Well, a 250-cubic-inch six and a 255-cubic-inch eight are almost the same size, and the eight can actually get better gas mileage if it is better engineered.

The General Motors X cars use a 4-cylinder engine that is 2.5 liters and a 6-cylinder engine that is 2.8 liters. Now how much difference do you really think that makes if everything else is equal? Detroit is trying to convince people that the cars are mileage efficient by playing a numbers game with cylinders. Remember—

many race cars are only 4 cylinders but if they get 2 miles to the gallon they are doing well. What all this means is, there probably will not be much difference in the cars 5 years from now, if you make a careful choice today.

By the way, if you like to tinker with your auto, do your own tune-ups, adjust the carburetor, set the timing—if you do all those good things to your car, you better keep the one you have because you won't be able to do them on the new models. As with many things these days, this can be blamed on the federal government. Look at the National Highway Traffic Safety Administration and the Environmental Protection Agency for many of the problems amateur mechanics run into. Acting at the behest of the U.S. Congress, the two bodies issued requirements that led to the sealing of automobile engines. The first of these requirements is the Corporate Average Fuel Economy Standard—the "CAFE standard." The second is the Clean Air Act. By demanding both fuel economy and cleaner exhaust, the government is forcing the auto manufacturers to build precision power plants that self-adjust for every variable. Human error is the most prevalent and harmful of the variables, so it is the first that must be eliminated. Most cars being built right now have carburetors you cannot touch. Soon they will have ignition systems you cannot touch. They already have sealed cooling systems and batteries.

No more careful adjusting of the idle-mixture screw, the choke setting, the idle speed, or the engine timing. Cars of the future will be manufactured with continuous electronic control of all engine functions. You can see this already on many cars with the three-way feedback catalytic system used by GM, Volvo, and Saab. The oxygen and exhaust-stream sensor sends signals to an electronically controlled carburetor or fuel-injection system to regulate the air–fuel mixture to achieve maximum fuel economy and complete combustion for a clean exhaust. Within the next decade, perhaps as early as 1985, these systems will evolve even further so that they have instantaneous regulation of ignition timing, valve openings and closings, and automatic engine start-up and shut-down, as well as individual cylinder start-up and shut-down.

These changes are on the drawing board, coming your way soon, and all mean that when you have a problem, you will not be able to fix it at home.

If you keep up with automotive publications or popular scientific magazines, you will have read about those wonderful scientific breakthroughs—the Stirling engine, gas turbines, and the electric cars. Although the federal government has helped fund some of the research into new power sources, and although government officials have called for the reinvention of the automobile, progress cannot be legislated. You cannot make a law that calls for a scientific or engineering breakthrough.

Ford has given up on the Stirling engine because of many engineering problems. In Europe, there is an Opel Rekord running around with a Stirling engine. At this writing, it has been on the road for about a year, the mileage is better than a comparable diesel, the air pollution beats the standards of the future, and it sounds like a dream come true. Right? Not right. The people behind the experimental car say they still have a long way to go. Whether it will hold up is the first problem, and that will take a lot more road experience to determine. Then comes the expense of many of the materials used in the Stirling. On top of this, the amount of time required to retool manufacturing facilities to an entirely new engine means that even if the engine meets all performance requirements it could not be brought to the market until 1990 or later.

The gas turbine was introduced by Chrysler in cars that were tried out across the country in the early sixties. Andy Granatelli was ruled off the Indy race track with his lightning-fast turbines, so what happened? Well, what happened was that turbines still cannot be made to run a car efficiently. They can go fast, and larger ones develop tremendous power, yet so far no one has managed to make a small one that runs well, holds up, and can be manufactured at a reasonable cost. Because of the tremendous heat generated by the turbine, special ceramic linings must be created to line many of the interior parts. Special alloys are needed for others. So far, these ceramics do not exist at a price that can make a turbine car practical. At the same time, turbines, although they are fuel-efficient at high speeds, are very poor on fuel at low speeds and actually are generally poor performers at low speeds. This means that at low speed, acceleration, and deceleration, the engine itself must be kept

15

running at high speeds. Obviously, this is very inefficient for normal city driving.

The government admits that turbines are a long way off, even though their high cost could be offset by their long life. An alternative, of course, would be a new fuel or a new source of oil. These possibilities will be brought out in another chapter. For the moment, suffice it to say that the "breakthroughs" presently being talked about are either too expensive or good enough only as temporary solutions. No one has a total answer—a fuel-efficient, safe, long-lasting automobile.

BUYING YOUR CAR WITHOUT PAIN

Chapter 1

THE CAR OF YOUR DREAMS

The most important part of buying a car takes place in your own home. It's there that you will decide exactly what you need to carry you down the highway of life in a style you can afford. New-car showrooms and used-car lots are designed to dazzle you into spending as much as possible as quickly as possible, and the smiling salesperson with lollipops for the kids only has a commission in mind. How then do you buy the car of your dreams and make sure it doesn't turn out to be a nightmare?

Four major companies in the United States turn out 13 different makes of cars. Each make has at least five models; Chevrolet has nine different models with a number of different trim levels and styles within each model line. Add to this the 30 or so foreign makes entering the country daily and about a hundred different companies turning out specialty sports cars, 4-wheel-drive vehicles, custom vans and recreational vehicles, along with limousines and custom-made convertibles, and you have the wide range of vehicles that the American car buyer is faced with in making a decision on just one that he or she must live with for the next 2, 5, 10, or 20 years.

The last two numbers are new to American car buyers. In this country, the usual new car buyer has expected to unload in two or three years and buy another car. The watchword has been, Let somebody else have the thing when it starts to give you problems. Today, however, the story is different, with the price of cars now averaging over $7,000 and heading upward. More and more car loans are being stretched over 4 years instead of 3, and people are beginning to think more like Europeans—that it's smart to buy the car that fits your needs now and for the next 10 years, then keep it running for at least that long.

How Do You Choose?

In the quiet of your own home you must decide exactly what size car you should have and how much you can spend. Decide whether your arthritis will allow you to roll the windows up and down yourself, or whether you need power windows. Will an AM-FM radio satisfy your inner need for music wherever you go, or must you be able to choose your own music via a cassette or 8-track tape unit? Can you hear just as well with one speaker or must you have four blasting at you?

We will go into what options you should have later on. For right now, begin to consider that some options increase the dollar *value* of the car, while others only increase the dollar *cost*. And many can be added more cheaply by after-market sources than by getting them from the dealer when you buy the car.

Size First let's deal with the size of the car you want. Many people today are looking fearfully at the gasoline situation and immediately setting their sights on the subcompact car—the tiny cars that you see more and more. Small they are, and most are fairly fuel-efficient, but they are not necessarily inexpensive. The cost of materials is one of the least significant factors when figuring how much it costs to build a car. The number of parts that must be manufactured, regardless of their size, and the quality of those parts are more important to the cost of the car. In other words, the small car may have just as many parts as the large car, and the cost of making them may be just as high, so its price may be within a couple of hundred dollars of the large car's price.

With the technical advances of today's cars and the weight reductions in the larger cars, fuel savings of small cars may not be worth their cost in comfort and convenience.

20

Subcompacts Most subcompacts have 4-cylinder engines and work best with manual 4- or 5-speed transmissions. They seat 4 people, but in many cases, the 2 in the rear are cramped, and in the case of the 2-door coupes the folks in the backseat had better be children or elves.

The fact that your children fit in the backseat today may not be reason enough to buy the subcompact if you intend to keep it 5 or 6 years or longer. Children have a nasty habit of growing, while a subcompact car is as large as it will ever be. Those vacation trips can be a mess when you can't fit all the luggage in the car along with the 2 kids and the dog.

Another item to remember is that those mileage figures on the window sticker are based on 2 people of average weight traveling in the car after it has warmed up. If you regularly carry several passengers and do a lot of stop-and-go short-trip driving, a small car may deliver very little more mileage than a larger, more comfortable one.

This seems to be a message that is hard to get across to the public. In simple terms, it takes a certain amount of energy to move a set amount of weight a certain distance. Add to this the fact that speed also affects how much gasoline is used and that the number of stops and starts must also be counted in, and you can see that determining economical gas mileage is a lot more involved than just deciding to buy a small car.

Perhaps this fact can be brought home more clearly by this true story. On my radio program in New York a caller said he was getting only 9 or 10 miles to the gallon in a Chevy Chevette. He said the Chevrolet people had tested the car and claimed he was getting better than 20 miles a gallon, but his bills from the service station told a different story. The man was ready to go to court but wanted an outside opinion. Since I was to be in New York for several days on business, I made an appointment to meet the man and test drive the car. He turned out to be a friendly young man with a business in Brooklyn and an earnest desire to get what he paid for without cheating anyone. He admitted the car had been trouble-free, but it just was not giving him the mileage he had been led to expect. We filled the car at a service station he habitually used and began our trek. I had several stops to make and at one point the car was left at idle while he made a phone call from a public booth and at another place we let the double-parked car idle while I looked in a store window. We put about 40 miles on the car in two hours and then filled it up again. The tank took less than 2 gallons, meaning better than 20 miles to the gallon. Now came the red face and the protestations that this was what happened when the Chevy people tested the car too, yet when he paid the bills it averaged out to 9 miles to the gallon. What was he doing wrong?

We started to discuss exactly how he used the car. The scenario went like this: He would drive to his place of business in the morning with his wife, a distance of a couple of miles. A few hours later, he would drive to his other store, another 2 or 3 miles, and he might, later in the day, drive to a third store operated by a relative. Trips between the three stores and suppliers, plus deliveries and pickups, all over short distances, were the main uses for the car, and the engine rarely had a chance to warm up. This meant that 90% of the time the car was driving with the automatic choke on because it did only stop-and-start city driving. In many cases, there was a second person or some merchandise in the car—extra weight. These things explained the low mileage. Running with the choke on costs a third or more of your gas mileage alone.

The gentleman was not happy, but he agreed it would be foolhardy to attempt to sue Chevrolet for the car's poor mileage. His mistake was in assuming the window sticker meant high mileage under all conditions. The fact is, the window sticker indicates mileage under ideal conditions.

What does this mean to you? Only that buying a small car may be the best thing for you, but you should weigh all pertinent factors. Subcompacts can also cost more new than compacts or even large cars.

As long as subcompacts are in demand, you won't get a price break from the dealer. And in some cases dealers charge more than the sticker price for them. They accomplish this by adding various handling and service charges and demanding that the buyer add all kinds of dealer-installed options.

The price difference between a Volkswagen Rabbit and a Chevy Malibu could easily be $2,000, and the mileage difference might be 15 miles to the gallon. With gas selling at $1.50 a gallon, that means you would have to travel quite a distance before you make up the $2,000 difference. In case you have misplaced your calculator, $2,000 buys 1,300 gallons of gasoline, and at 20 miles to the gallon when you buy the cheaper car, you get 26,000 miles free. Repeat: 26,000 *free* miles. For the average driver, that is over 2 years of driving free.

Think it over. By buying the cheaper car that gets lower mileage, you get the first 2 years of gasoline free. You also get a larger, more comfortable vehicle that will cost less to service because it was made in Detroit.

If you finance your car, the saving will also show up in less interest paid on the lower-priced car.

This means the automobile world has turned upside down. Many small cars cost more than large cars, and this year's models are more expensive than ever. The new subcompacts are higher priced than before, but that's nothing new. They have been pricing cars higher every year for the past 20 years. The fact is the X Cars from General Motors have gone up 45% in price since first introduced 2½ years ago. That means it is not unheard of to buy an X Car with a lot of equipment on it for over $10,000. And Chrysler comes out with the K Car in competition. Do they lower the price? No. The K Car can be bought for as high as $11,000, fully equipped.

In Detroit, Chrysler, GM, Ford, and the rest have spent billions, some say as high as $80 billion, downsizing their autos. They have to get that money back. Where? In the cars that sell best. What cars sell best? Small cars. At least for now. In the long run, the public may decide that the large car is the better value for the money. If you can get room and comfort at the sacrifice of just a few miles per gallon, chances are you will buy that larger car. Wouldn't it be strange, after spending all these billions of dollars if Detroit found it priced itself out of the small-car market, sending many people back to the big cars? Wouldn't that upset the federal government, which wants everyone to save fuel with small cars?

Even though people continue to talk about downsizing, buying smaller cars, and getting better gas mileage, when they walk into the showroom that is not what they ask for.

The pocketbook says buy Chevette, Escort, Omni, K Car, X Car, but deep down you still like that Cadillac, Lincoln, Imperial. So what do you do? Apparently, as a normal American buyer, you load up the little car with big-car options. You want gas economy, yet you turn around and say you want an automatic transmission, air conditioning, power brakes, power steering, all of which rob gas mileage. These features all work off belts from the engine, taking away horsepower and gas mileage.

General Motors estimates that a fourth of its Chevettes are ordered with all the options.

The Ford Motor Company has a story much the same on the new subcompacts, the Escort and Lynx. Ford corporate spokespeople say subcompacts have never before been offered with so many upscale options. Ford thinks that the Americans' taste for options will give it the marketplace advantage. But Chrysler is not going to be left behind. The K Car can also be had with every option you can imagine which means the American driver wants good mileage as long as he or she can still steer with one finger, brake with one toe, and cruise the highway in complete air-conditioned comfort. The typical driver will sacrifice as much gas mileage as necessary for this kind of comfort.

The subcompact may be the perfect car for you, but before you buy it, be sure it fits all your needs and your budget.

By the way, you will note we have not differentiated between domestic and foreign cars. The Detroit boys are putting out cars in direct competition with the foreign makers and they should not be ignored. The mystique of the foreign car wears off very quickly when you begin to compare repair charges after 40,000 or 50,000 miles.

The Compact Car   This size generally carries 5 or 6 people and is gaining more and more acceptance as a reasonable compromise for the family that wants the economy of the 4- or 6-cylinder engine without giving up the comfort of the larger car. American compacts can easily handle automatic transmissions and air conditioning, whereas the foreign equivalents are, in most cases, much higher priced than Detroit models. This is offset somewhat by their generally higher mileage and a higher grade of technology. The technology, fit, and finish of the imported cars is undoubtedly better than those of American counterparts, but technology is expensive both in the initial price and later repairs. The sports-car-type ride and acceleration available in many of these cars is a high-priced luxury to someone who does only city driving and carries the family on most long drives. Nevertheless, foreign cars should not be overlooked. If you can afford them, they can bring back a thrill to driving that you have not had since you borrowed your friend's MG back in the 1950s. Besides the fine motoring experience, they still carry four people comfortably and a fifth with a little squeeze, plus a full complement of luggage.

Big Cars   Next come the big cars, or what is left of the big cars these days. Gone are the last of the mile-long behemoths, replaced by the downsized versions that weigh less, turn more easily, use less gas, and take up only one parking place at a time. Smaller cars do everything big ones did and do it better, but they do not impress the guys at the corner bar half as much as the old ones did. The mileage on today's big cars is less than on subcompacts and compacts, but their comfort level is much higher, and they can carry the whole team with its equipment to the Little League field.

Specialty Cars   The final category of automobile on the market is the specialty car. Strangely enough, these 2-door coupes, generally get the poorest mileage, carry 2 people in comfort and 2 more in agony, are flashy and overpriced, and sell better than most of the other styles.

Since the early 1950s, when the auto makers studied the psychology of the car buyer and came up with *the* contradiction on wheels—the hardtop convertible—the buying public has been plunking down extra bucks for less car and more flash.

The big thinkers in Detroit discovered that more people entered the showroom because of a gorgeous white convertible in the window than to look over the gray 4-door sedan better suited to wallet and family needs. But Momma would not think of allowing the kids to ride in the back of an open car, and weren't they cold in the winter, and besides, Fred, you are not 18 anymore.

Enter design engineers in concert with psychology students and out comes the hardtop convertible. With all the looks and flash of a rag top, but the roof is steel—and Harriet is satisfied if Fred drops a few extra bucks to satisfy his teenaged ego, because she likes a little flash too, and besides, all her main objections have been met.

The hardtop quickly became the hottest style on the road, leading to Mustangs, Thunderbirds, Eldorados, Monte Carlos, ad infinitum.

These cars are not the best buys, and lately, with the air-pollution equipment and unleaded gasoline, they are neither the fastest nor the best handling. Nevertheless, they continue to sell and sell well.

Body Style Rounding out your choices are the various body styles with the above categories. Virtually all the cars, regardless of size, come in 2-door or 4-door models, and many with hatchbacks. The choice here is yours. Four-doors are much more convenient for family use, while 2-doors generally are easier for a large driver to get in and out of. The 2-doors are generally considered more sporty, and many have less room in the rear seats. At times, the hatchback can be an invitation to thieves when the storage compartment is not covered, but, in general, it is a very convenient extra.

What Options?

By now, in the privacy of your own home, you have begun to narrow down your choices to 3 or 4 models and makes. It's time to look at the options list, which can add thousands of dollars to the price of your dreamboat if you are not careful.

First, let's look at *engines*. Detroit continues to offer several different powerplants for most of its cars, including 4-, 6-, and 8-cylinder models, turbocharging and diesel powerplants.

You must decide where your priorities lie. The smallest engine available is generally adequate for everyday, around-town driving, but it loses its mileage edge if you expect to carry large loads often. If you regularly carry a trailer, a larger engine is a must, along with a heavy-duty suspension and cooling package.

• *Turbochargers*—add about $1,000 to the price of a car, give it more kick in the midrange without using extra gas, but make the car liable to just that many more problems down the road a piece.
• *Diesel engines*—are being touted for their great mileage and, indeed, they do give the best mileage per cubic inch of displacement

of any engine available. They are, however, generally harder to start, especially in cold weather, noisier, smellier, and slower to accelerate. They also require servicing more often than the gasoline engine. Finding a diesel fuel in your neighborhood can also be a problem and finding a diesel mechanic can be a real chore.

• *Transmissions*—come in as many variations as engines, and the choices again depend on who is using the car, and for what purpose. Manual transmissions are better on fuel, but automatics are easier for stop-and-go city driving. Overdrive or 5-speed transmissions will add miles to the gallon on the road, but are not much use in town. Domestic manual transmissions are generally not as easy to use as those on foreign cars, and recently the quality of the automatics has left something to be desired.

• *Power steering*—makes things a lot easier in the city where parking is a problem. It usually has a lower ratio, meaning that there are fewer turns of the wheel from one direction to the other. This makes the car more agile and faster to respond. These qualities are important, especially with a large car. But you will lose some road feel with power steering.

• *Power brakes*—are exactly what the name implies. Rather than just your muscle to stop the car, a power assist is added. Most cars have power brakes as standard. Where they are not standard, try a car without them. You may find it brakes easily enough—and save a few dollars.

• *Air conditioning*—is always an extra, except on the most expensive cars. Try to get a factory-installed unit. Dealer add-ons are generally not as good. Although air conditioning can cost as much as 4 miles to the gallon on a hot day, a car with air conditioning is worth more at trade-in time or when you go to sell it. (The same is true of cars with power steering and brakes.) Fancy climate-control units generally cost more and break down more often. Manual-control air conditioning does the job just as well with fewer headaches.

Air conditioning also helps cut down on driver fatigue on long summer trips. Tinted glass is a must with air conditioning on most cars, but for some people with eye trouble, clear glass may be preferable.

• The *rear defroster*—or defogger is another absolutely essential item. Unless you live in a deserted desert, you will appreciate being able to see out the rear window, whatever the weather. In some states, a rear defroster is mandatory. It should be in all states.

• *Extras*—The above options are the most important choices. What follows are extras that you may or may not want or need. Remember, most American cars have enough extras to double the price before you're finished.

Let's Start with Trim Items

The vinyl roof, half roof, or any other roof configuration is basically useless. If it loses its watertightness over the years, rust will begin to form under it, and the resulting repair job can be very expensive. Some expensive cars make fancy padded roofs as part of a special trim package. The sensible thing to do is to pass the package up and in some cases save a couple of thousand dollars. From what I see on the road, more and more people seem to be doing this, and the cars actually look better for it. This indicates that resale value will not be harmed by the lack of the roof blanket, which was not true several years ago when so-called skin tops were considered unstylish.

• *Special sport paint jobs?* In some cases, in order to get certain engines, handling packages, or other features that you might want for performance, you must also take a fancy paint job with decals and striping and other doodads. If possible, do without the paint, leave off as much tape and decal work as you can. If you like pinstriping, get the painted kind. Not the tape. Tape is just going to peel off after a while and look a mess.

• Special limited-edition cars with fancy decorations and the like are sometimes bought in the hope that they will become collector's items. Be careful. The Corvette Indy Pace Car Replica, which is a close match for the one that was used at the Indianapolis 500, will be a collector's item. On the other hand, the Mustang Pace Car Replica of 1979 was totally different from the actual pace car. The one sold by the Ford dealers was a turbocharged 4-cylinder engine, while the one used at Indianapolis was a specially prepared 8-cylinder car. The replica will probably not have much value as a collector's item.

• Side moldings for the body and bumper protectors are worthwhile.

Both are plastic or rubber and prevent little nicks in the paint from the car doors opening beside you, and other cars' bumpers cannot climb over yours if you have front and rear bumper guards. Full-width rubber facings on the bumpers also offer protection.

• Most cars today offer a wide selection of seats and seat fabrics. The power seat usually offers more positions for comfort but, of course, is more complicated and is one more draw on the battery and electrical system. A power seat combined with the tilt steering wheel can make a vehicle easier to get in and out of and adjusts easily to different drivers. Usually, it also comes as a split front bench or bucket seat, which means the two sides in front can be adjusted differently, providing more comfort for both passengers in the front and, possibly, even in the back.

• Sometimes the full bench seat in larger cars makes it possible to seat three in the front, but this, generally, means crowding and poor safety conditions. Bucket seats are the most secure, offering support at the sides as well as the back. When auto makers are forced to go to passive restraints, that is, belts that automatically grab you as you get in, the bucket and split bench will probably be the only seats offered except on cars equipped with air bags at extra cost.

• Solid vinyl seat covering is very hot in the summer. Perforated vinyl and fabric are cooler but harder to keep clean.

• Tires usually are offered in a wide range of types. Get radials. They offer longer life and better mileage. If you live in an area where there is snow in the winter, an all-season radial is excellent.

• Undercoating and rustproofing are big items today, with a lot of advertising going into them. Undercoating is an absolute necessity. Rustproofing will add weight yet is still a good option on most cars. Along with the various forms of polymer finishes offered to protect the paint, be aware that these items have a large dealer markup, and you can bargain on their cost. Also be aware that these extras should come with their own warranties. How well these finishes are applied is more important than brand names. But make sure that they are done properly or they are useless. (We will be talking more about these in a later chapter.)

• Wipers that can pause between strokes and rear-window wipers or air deflectors on hatchbacks and station wagons are also good options to maintain rear visibility.

• A car with obstructed view to the rear or side because of fancy rear window posts should have a right side mirror, and you should learn to use it when driving. Fancy sport mirrors are useless or, at most, no more useful than plain mirrors.

• Courtesy lights, power windows, power door locks, sun roofs, and T-roofs are just a matter of personal preference. They all have drawbacks or cost extra and can be done without.

• We have not talked about the radio, and for good reason. People who are satisfied with an ordinary radio, perhaps an AM-FM, will be happy with what the dealer has to offer from the factory. If you are a real audio buff, however, you probably want to add the sound system afterward, picking and choosing from the 30 or so brands available at the specialty audio stores rather than the few offered by the dealer. Prices vary from $50 to over $1,000, and since you're the one who must live with it, let your ears and pocketbook be your guide.

Chapter 2

AT THE DEALER, OR GAMESMANSHIP WITH A VENGEANCE

Dealers and Deals

By now you know what size car you want and what options you want on it. It remains to decide what make and where to buy it. Again, this choice ought to be made in your own living room. Read all you can about the various makes. Use consumer magazines, car magazines, and any other information you can find, but remember that the people testing the cars may be rating different things. The consumer magazine may be looking at general serviceability and resale value, while the auto buff magazine wants performance and style. You want something in between the dull 4-door "el strippo model" and the $30,000 "exoticar" extolled by the sports car mag.

Consider carefully what you will use the car for, not just now but 5 years from now.

Don't lock yourself into a single make. Remember that, in many cases, Detroit builds the same car under several names—Ford Fairmount and Mercury Zephyr, Chevy Malibu, Olds Cutlass,

Pontiac Le Mans and Buick Century, Plymouth Volaré and Dodge Aspen, etc. This gives you several dealers to talk to about virtually the same car. You may be able to find a dealer who is nearer to your home, who has a good reputation, or who offers a better deal.

Always shop around, but don't forget that the dealer can be just as important as the make of car. Giving a reputable dealer an extra hundred or two for a car can mean a great savings in aggravation in the long run. Remember other things, too. Some dealers will give you a loaner when your car is being serviced. A dealer who is closer to your home can mean a great savings in time and effort when you need service.

Dealers who have your car in stock will probably make you a better deal than those who have to order what you want. This is because they are paying interest on the money borrowed to stock the car. They also cannot allow unsold cars to stand around and take up valuable space.

Sometimes a dealer will make you a much better deal on a car in stock that may have more equipment on it than you want. It could pay to take the loaded car if the price is close enough to the stripped model you want. For instance, I was offered a Mustang Pace Car with a sticker price of over $9,000 for just over $7,500. Another Mustang with loads of equipment but with a sticker price of only $7,400 was discounted to $6,800. I could have gotten the highest priced model for just $700 more than a car with a sticker price of $1,600 less. The reason was simple. The dealer felt he had a better chance of selling the lower-priced car than the top-of-the-line Pace Car Replica.

In some cases, it pays to buy a less popular model car, especially if you intend to keep it for 5 or more years. After 5 years, the resale value of most cars depends more on condition than on the model. The amazing thing that has happened in the past year is the failure of the large cars to sell in this country. This has led to the strange phenomenon of large cars selling for hundreds of dollars less than similarly equipped compacts or subcompacts.

Which is not to say you should run out and buy a large car. It is to point out that there are bargains to be had if you shop. Sometimes it pays to buy a car at model-change time. Buying last year's car can always save you money. Again, this is only true if you intend to keep the car for 5 years or more. Because the car has a built-in double depreciation, you would lose as much as you saved if you sold the car or traded it before it was 5 years old.

What is a double depreciation? Simply stated, any car loses value the minute it rolls out of the dealer's lot and becomes a used car. And it depreciates again when the next year's models appear. When you buy last year's model at the end of the year, those two depreciations take place at the same time.

Choosing the Right Dealer

Every year in the United States, some 25 to 30 million people buy cars. Ten million buy them new, and the rest settle for used cars. Of this number, perhaps 10% know how to deal with the car salesman. Americans lose what amounts to billions of dollars on the deals they make. They settle for add-ons and options they really do not want or need. Worst of all, they spend what amounts to $400 million a year on something called "dealer preparation." First, this so-called dealer preparation is covered in the sticker price of the car, and, second, most dealers do not do it anyway.

Foreign-car dealers with hot-selling items are the most notorious in this regard. In some cases, state attorney generals have filed suit against both distributors and dealers for tacking on special paint sealers and rustproofers and calling them standard equipment at an extra cost. When a salesman starts to add on costs over and above the factory sticker, head for the door. Do not dicker or bargain or anything else. Head for the door, and see how fast the preparation charges disappear.

Remember that other dealers sell the same make, and one of them will be ready to deal properly on the car you want.

This brings us to another item—the availability of makes and dealers. It has already been mentioned about some of the things you should look for as far as location and reputation. Sometimes in small towns, however, there are very few dealers, and some even carry more than one brand of car. In these cases, it is hard to bargain. They are the only game in town, and they pretty much get whatever they ask for on their cars.

In such a situation, pick the dealer with the best service reputation. In a small town, the only bargaining tools you have are (1) to indicate you will wait until next year to buy or (2) to threaten to buy a different brand.

The small-town dealer and the small dealer in a larger city are totally different animals. Both will have smaller inventories, fewer models from which to choose, smaller service departments, fewer salespeople, fewer mechanics, and generally a lower overhead. The difference is that the small-town dealer has little competition while the small dealer in the larger city is battling the big boys and eventually would like to be one of the big boys. That dealer may deal closer to the vest to make you happy and may try to give better service for the same reason. To become bigger, he needs to build up a satisfied clientele that keeps coming back and also spreads the word. He depends on word of mouth because he cannot afford to spend a great deal of money on advertising.

Be careful of one thing. A small dealer who has always been small and doesn't seem to be getting larger may be lacking in some facet of the business—poor service, poor deals, bad attitude, and so forth.

In many cases, large does not mean better. Some large dealers got there strictly on volume sales, and their service may be nonexistent. Once you have purchased the car, they may ignore you and any problems you have. You may find that their service charges are very high in order to offset the low sales price on the car. When you come in for the scheduled maintenance items to keep your warranty in effect, you may discover that the called-for oil change and general checkup cost $25 to $50 more than the average garage would charge for the same work. If your warranty calls for two such visits to the dealer, he has made back $50 or $100 of that good deal he gave you.

Does it sound as if the buyer is caught in a double bind? True, but choosing a dealer really boils down to two things. Price and reputation. Talk to people who have dealt with him and used his service. Then see what his best deal is. Going through this process with two or three dealers should find you one with whom you can do business.

Most dealers try to bring you in with advertising. Once you come through the door, you are on their turf, and the advertising that enticed you may or may not describe what the dealer actually has for sale.

The old bait-and-switch is pretty much dead, but you still have to look out for it. This means that a particular car model is advertised at a very low price, but when you arrive to buy it, either it doesn't exist at all or the guy before you just bought the last one. Mostly, bait-and-switch has been changed over to the "el strippo." The dealer stocks the car advertised at a low price, but it has absolutely no options; none of the amenities you want or like. It is really the kind of car companies buy for their fleets of delivery vehicles or the like. You discover that if you want some of the creature comforts, you have to pay more.

With the skyrocketing price of cars today, many dealers advertise monthly payments. Such low payments look good, but the fine print will call for a large downpayment or a much longer payment term than normal. It also may indicate this price is for "qualified buyers only," which means only people with top-grade credit.

Tip: Having been in the advertising business for many years, the best advice I can give is to point out that what one dealer can do, they all can do. No dealer beats everyone, no dealer can make a better deal, no dealer can be what all those adjectives in his ads say. When scanning the ads for the best bet, cross out all the words like "super," "fantastic," "great," "beautiful," etc. In used car ads, disregard words like "select," "reconditioned," "extra clean," etc.

Tricks of the Car Trade   A number of books on the market give the factory-cost prices on cars, and some of the consumer publications do the same. You should arm yourself with these figures before you go out to shop for your car. To the base factory price, add $200 or $300 in profit for the dealer on reasonably popular models, less on models that are not moving well, and probably more on the cars that are selling well.

Arming yourself with the figures is all important. You may consider yourself a real dyed-in-the-wool horse trader, but that guy in the auto showroom spends his life making profitable car deals. He is the shark and you are the minnow, regardless of how smart you may think you are. His livelihood depends on making car sales that make money. You can never beat him, but you can hold him to a draw. That is, you can get the best possible deal, and he can get a reasonable profit.

Low-balling   I have mentioned that buying a car from stock might get you a good deal because the dealer wants to move the cars on the lot. They are costing the business money. There are, however, some advantages to the factory order. You will get just the car you want in the color you like, with options you believe you need. You also have time to sell your present car while you are waiting for the new one. This might get you an extra few dollars when you eliminate the trade-in and deal on a cash basis. The problem with the factory order is that you are now off the market and at the dealer's mercy. The dealer may have in fine print the fact that price increases that occur while you await delivery will be added to the final price. If your trade goes down in value, you may have to make up the difference or, worst of all, you may have been low-balled.

This is a subtle trick that is hard to prove. The dealer has made you a spectacular deal, and now you are waiting for the car. You have a buyer lined up for your old one, and you wait. You call the dealer, and he says, "Be patient." He tells you there was a snafu on the order. He tells you they sent through the wrong car. He tells you anything, then he invites you in or you just drop in to see what is going on. Now he has you. Your car may get there in a few weeks, but look at this baby that just came in. It is only a few hundred dollars more than the one you ordered, and you can have it right now.

The way around this trap is to have the dealer write on the order exactly how long you must wait with a notation that if the car is not in by that time, he must refund your deposit. If he won't do this, leave and do not look back.

If, when you arrive at the dealer's to pick up your car, the dealer indicates the price of the car went up and this is not covered in the fine print of the contract, demand your deposit back and leave. If he tries to change the price of your trade-in and this is not covered by the fine print, demand your deposit and leave.

It might even be a good idea to find another dealer and a car a week before your car is due to arrive. This way, if the dealer you ordered from starts to play games, you have a back-up car to buy and are not tempted to give in.

"Under Pricing" Watch out for the dealer who claims he will sell a car below factory invoice. The only way this can be done is with a repossession, a factory executive car or a demonstrator. In other words, you are being offered a used car that may not have the full factory warranty and may have more miles than shown on the odometer.

If a dealer says he is selling a new car under invoice, he is lying. The invoice is a fake, and he is not to be trusted under any circumstances.

Pricing Trade-ins When you expect to trade in your old car as part of a deal, you must remember certain facts of life.

1. Your car has a certain value. The dealer knows that value—you should also. Your bank or insurance company will have the same trade books that the dealer uses to determine value. Check with them.
2. You love your car, the dealer does not. You know you have kept it in good shape, the dealer does not, nor does he care. That it has new tires or a new muffler is immaterial to the dealer. At best, you may get some mileage out of the fact that the cleaner your car is, the less the dealer will have to do to sell it.
3. The dealer will use every blemish on the car against you if you give him a chance.

If you stand by when he appraises the car he will point out every problem, sometimes in words, more often silently, letting you tick off in your mind the dollars that you just lost on the trade. Do not let him do it. Walk away while he appraises the car. Go back and re-examine the car you want to buy. Wander around the lot, clean your fingernails in the corner. Do not let him psych you into believing your car is worth less money. If he asks you to stand by while he inspects your car, simply tell him you see the car every day and you do not have to look at it again. You want to look at his merchandise again.

Another gimmick is to tell you how long it took to sell another used car just like yours, how bad this particular car was, and so on. The story may or may not be true, but that should not affect your bargaining position. You know what the car is worth because you checked it out. Negotiate from that standpoint and no other.

Beating the Sales Pitch All salespeople have a canned, rehearsed selling pitch. They try to control the entire transaction and make it tough for you to say no at the end. They batter you with questions, and they answer your question with a question. They try to make you commit yourself by turning your questions around. You inquire, "Will you throw in the floor mats?" and the salesperson's response may be, "Will you buy tonight if I throw in the floor mats?" He has not answered the question, he has only asked you to buy the car. You must learn to use the same technique. If you answer yes or no, you have ended the negotiations. Your answer should be along these lines: "If I decide to buy the car, I would want you to throw in the floor mats. Will you do that?"

You have wiggled off the hook and asked the question again. If *you* ask the questions, *you* control the situation.

In some cases, when the salesperson asks you a question, ignore it. Act as if you did not hear it and ask a question that has nothing to do with his. Do anything to break the pattern.

Remember, you have one great advantage over the salesman. At any time, you can get up and leave. Do not be afraid to do it.

One of the biggest ploys is to deal with a customer on the basis of monthly payments instead of total price. Many people actually tell a salesperson how much they can afford each month, and he proceeds to tailor a sale for their budget—not to save the customer money, but to get every last cent of the car money available. He will stretch payments to 4 years instead of 3 seemingly to lower the payments. In reality, he has increased the dealer's kickback from the finance company. He will try to tack the insurance payment on to the car payment. Again, he has landed the dealer another commission.

He will quote you a low price if he feels you're just shopping, and when you return to get that price, the car you wanted is gone, but he happens to have one just a little higher priced. He will leave you in order to get special permission from the sales manager to lower the price another $100. When he comes back, he says he just got reamed out because the original price he offered you was $200 too low. Then, in comes the sales manager. Because his salesperson said so, you may have the original price just so you will not think badly of him. Aren't you lucky? The sales manager just offered to give you the car at the same price the salesperson quoted instead of raising it $200, but you better grab it because if you don't that price will not be available tomorrow.

Another tried-and-true sales ploy is to allow a husband and wife to sit alone in the office while the salesperson checks on something. What is being checked on is the couple's conversation while he is gone. It is illegal, but the office is bugged. He wants to see how close to a sale he is. He wants to know if the last price discussed is what they are ready to pay if he does not come down further. He wants to see whether the wife or the husband is the dominant partner, and how the dominant one feels about the deal in order to know which of two he has to sell. If one person happens to chuckle and say he or she would have paid $200 more for the car, you can bet he will come back and tell the couple he made a $200 mistake.

Tip: Never tell a salesperson you are going to pay cash. If he knows that he will attempt to get more profit out of the sale because he is losing the finance commission.

Beating Deal-Closing Techniques   James Ross, a former car salesperson, in his book *How to Buy A Car,* talks of moves that may be used in trying to close a deal with you.

• A salesperson may try to use sympathy. Make you feel sorry for him. Sales are down, have not been making enough money to support my family, etc., etc. The only sympathy you should have when buying a car is for you, your own spouse, and/or your pocketbook.
• Another close involves a company-sponsored or factory-sponsored contest or bonus. The factory does sponsor such contests, and salespeople have found it is a great idea to tell somebody, "I only need one more sale to win a trip to Hawaii." Since you are not going on the trip, you really do not care if he goes to Hawaii.
• Sometimes the salesperson wants to make you feel sorry for yourself and convince you the only way to ease your sorrow is to buy his car. "You owe it to yourself," he assures you. What you do owe yourself is a lower monthly payment not a high one, less of a burden on your budget, and a car that fits your needs, not the car the salesperson thinks you ought to have.

• Be wary when a salesperson tells you, "I am mad at my boss, and I don't care if this company makes any money or not, so I am going to give you the highest discount anybody ever got here." Please realize that the salesperson does not decide what the final discount is. The boss is going to make the decision, and the salesperson is paid based on the gross profit on the car. If he gives you that big discount, he is handing out his own money. His being angry with his boss is not going to get you a better deal. He might turn that around and say, "My boss is in a good mood today, so we'll have no trouble getting you the trade allowance you want. The books say your car is worth $3,000, but I'm going to get you the $3,300 you want."

Forget it. The sales manager looks at the numbers with detached emotion: profit is profit, loss is loss, and he is going to write the deal that he thinks will entice you to buy the car and get him his profit.

• The salesperson may get chummy with you. "Can I talk to you like a brother? If you were my brother, I'd give you this advice." And he goes on to advise you. Or he might say, "I am going to treat you like my own sister, give you the same deal I would give her."

It is a great way to relieve doubt, to get you to believe that he's closing the credibility gap between you.

Be careful when somebody says he is going to treat you like a brother or sister.

• When a salesperson says, "I am new in this business," look out. Any veteran salesman might use that line to make you lower your guard. If you know you are dealing with a 15-year veteran salesman, you are more likely to realize that you're dealing with a pro and resist the sales pitch. Conversely, you might tend to feel relaxed around a novice. You think you can handle him, and are unprepared to do real battle. Believe me, if this person is on a new- or used-car showroom floor, he knows how to sell. If he started yesterday or 7,700 yesterdays ago, you must do battle with him. He makes his living selling.

• Another gimmick is the "other customer strategy"—the attempt to create urgency. "Buy this car today because another person is interested in it." The other person, of course, is the sales manager or another salesperson. The scenario might work like this. The phone rings. "Yes, Mr. Jones, I still have that car in stock. As a matter of fact, I have another person sitting here thinking of buying, how soon can you get here?" The coincidence of somebody calling about the same car you want while you are sitting in the room is stretching it a bit far. Naturally, there is no other person. You may not want to lose the car, but don't let eagerness make you sign for it at a higher price.

There is nothing urgent about buying a car. There are enough dealers and cars for everyone.

• Another angle is to inform you the customer that the sales manager will sell the car the way you want it only if you buy today. "Come back tomorrow, you won't get the same deal." Your first instinct is, "If he'll sell it to me today for that price, he'll sell it to me tomorrow for the same price." To that logic the salesperson replies, "I've seen him do this before. Customer didn't believe he meant it, next day customer came back, and the sales manager refused to give the same price he quoted the day before. The sales manager wants your business today, not tomorrow."

If the sales manager can sell you that car today for a profit, he will sell it to you tomorrow for a profit, and the next day, 10 days from now, or 10 weeks from now.

• Let's talk about silence. A good salesperson asks the final questions. He asks you to buy the car, puts the paper in front of you, points to the dotted line and says, sign here, and then shuts up. First person to break the silence loses. If the salesman continues talking after he has pointed to that dotted line, he doesn't know how to sell. And if you don't change the subject, you have lost. It is a game played by every salesperson. If the silence fills the office long enough, you either walk out or sign. That is what the salesperson wants. After he has spent time with you, he can't afford to spend more time, and he wants you to sign or get out. It is up to you not to be intimidated by the silence.

Everybody thinks he or she is unique. You think when you go into that dealership, you are going to bargain in a unique fashion and will have objections to buying that are unique. But the salesperson has heard it all. You may say, we want to think about it, talk it over, let you know tomorrow; the salesperson's response, "What do you want to think about, talk over? If you need to talk anything over, I'll leave you here. Call me when you are ready."

Or you might state that you have to go home and talk it over with your spouse. The salesperson's response: "What do you have to talk over? Can't you make the decision now? Here's the phone. Call home now. Let's take the car over to your house and show it off. It will give you a chance to drive it again."

How about your objection that the price is too much? The salesperson assumes you don't know how much is too much, so he will ask, "Is it too high because you can't afford to spend that much, or because you can get a better price from another dealer?" If it is more than you can afford, he will try to switch you to a less expensive model. If another dealer can offer a better deal, he will attempt to beat it with amenities. You should pay more to get better service, salespeople, and so on.

All your excuses are rebutted in a manner that puts the salesperson in control. He will ferret out the real reason you want to leave without buying and force you to give another reason, another why not, until you run out of reasons. This technique is called "plugging up gopher holes."

When you really want to leave, you will find the "sleep on it" excuse very effective. Tell the salesperson you never buy without sleeping on it. He can hardly offer to let you sleep in the dealership overnight to reach your final decision. Another maneuver if you are with someone—spouse, fiancé, or friend—and need to get off the hook is simply to start an argument with your companion. Plan in advance to do so. It can be a lot of fun if you put on a good act. Few salespeople are going to butt into an argument. Begin with a simple situation—you like blue, she likes red—get into heavy differences of opinion, and then leave.

There is one possible way to short-circuit all the game playing. Once you have decided exactly what car you want and what equipment, and have researched the dealer's cost and retail price, you can make a flat offer. Your offer should be at least $200 over cost and probably nearer to $300 because the dealer has interest charges to pay on the car. Throw in the fact that you will let him do the financing if you plan to anyway. If the salesperson says he will take your offer, tell him to get the sales manager's approval right away and write up the deal. You can use this method only if you are not trading in a car and actually are ready to buy on the spot. The dealer may try to get you involved in negotiations anyway by making a counteroffer. Ignore the negotiations but haggle on any counteroffer within $100 of your first price. You usually can split the difference on any counteroffer.

Get Help if You Need It   There are now car-buying specialists who offer advice to prospective buyers. These consultants try to determine what car you should buy and then give you the price you should pay. Armed with this information, you then search for a dealer who will meet the suggested deal. It may well be an idea whose time has come.

Remember, no one can choose a car for you. You are the one who must live with it, drive it, suffer with it. It must be comfortable to you. If there are to be two or more drivers, they must all be relatively comfortable in the car. Test driving the car for a few minutes at the dealer's is really not enough. You should spend a while behind the wheel to get the real feeling of the car. If you have a friend or relative with a similar car, try to borrow it for a test drive. Otherwise, rent the car for a day from the dealer, or from one of the regular rental companies. It may cost a few dollars, but the outlay may save you years of frustration. Almost every make of car available in this country is offered for rent by one of the major rental companies.

Picking the Right Payment Plan

You have made a deal on your car, you are satisfied with what you got, and the dealer is pleased to sell it at the price you mutually agreed on. Now, how are you going to pay for it?

The long-term installment contract is a way of life today in the buying of a new car. You may not be aware that back in 1915 the Guarantee Securities Company of Toledo, Ohio, introduced the first auto-installment buying plan. General Motors Acceptance Corporation was number two. What has happened since then is that the length of payback has gone from 1 year to 2 years to 3 years, and a while ago the 48-month contract came to be the end all and be all, and now it has been replaced by a 5-year plan. This is caused by the increased average retail cost of cars—they run about $8,000 today—

and if prices keep going higher, the extended payback terms will stretch even more.

Actually, we are almost at the point where we are dealing with the British term "hire purchase," which means we hire the car and, eventually, if we pay out long enough, we will own it. Very few Americans have a car long enough to own it. They wind up turning around and putting together another "hire purchase" package before they have paid off the first one.

If you are thinking about taking one of these long-term contracts, figure out its APR (annual percentage rate). Then compute an average inflation rate by adding up the inflation rate for the last two quarters and the projected annual rate of inflation for the nation in the coming year. If the APR and your average inflation rate come close, consider the long-term contract. If inflation is significantly lower than the interest rate, choose the shortest term contract you can get with the highest monthly rates you can handle. (If the reverse is true, forget the whole thing because the country is in terrible trouble, and the economy is not going to be able to hold up through the next few years.)

The point is this: When the inflation rate is as high as the interest rate, you will find that you are paying back on a long contract with cheaper dollars. Otherwise, the shortest payback system you can get is worthwhile.

Leasing

Particularly in the last 2 years, many Americans are turning to leasing instead of buying. This is primarily because of the tremendous boost in the new car prices. Many folks who would like to buy a car are unable to come up with a large down payment, but they find they can still drive a new car by leasing it because leasing usually requires less of an initial cash outlay. Auto leasing is no more expensive than buying a new car when the lease is properly written. On the other hand, it is no cheaper, considering the total amount of money paid over the life of the agreement. Whether you lease or buy, the net amount you finance is nearly the same. Your decision to buy or lease a car depends on your financial condition and whether pride of ownership is important to you.

Leasing also has a new wrinkle. This is a combination leasing and buying, again very close to the British "hire purchase" system. It gives you the benefits of both owning and leasing a car, and its fine points really need to be explained in much detail. If you are interested in a combination, I suggest you contact local leasing companies.

A straight lease takes less of a down payment than buying, but you will need a better credit rating to meet most leasing-company standards. You must also have a particular income level, depending on the car being financed.

Before you decide to lease, you should understand that the payments during the length of the lease entitle you only to use an automobile; ownership remains with the lessor, and at the end of the agreement the leasing company takes the car back. The payments are based on estimates of the amount of depreciation over the term of the lease. There will be additional fees to operate the car, plus the leasing company's expected profit divided by the total number of months specified in the agreement.

The price you pay on a lease is based on several factors. Obviously, the initial cost of the car, the cost of financing the car, but it is also based on what the lessor thinks the car will be worth 2 or 3 years down the road at the end of the lease. The average car depreciates 3% per month in the first year. That's 36%. On the other hand, certain models depreciate as little as half of 1% per month, meaning only 6% in the first year. A low rate of depreciation means that, since the leasing company is going to wind up with the car after a 2- or 3-year lease, the lessor should calculate the package based on the fact that the car may be worth much more at the end of the 3 years than a comparable vehicle of another make or model. They can deduct that extra value from what they charge you.

Now let's put some names to it.

For instance, if you were leasing a $10,000 Cadillac, you would probably actually pay less than someone leasing a $9,000 Chrysler, despite the higher initial price. The reason is obvious. Cadillacs currently depreciate at a slower rate than Chryslers.

To give you an idea, one leasing company executive, Allen Mitchell, vice president of Executive Car Leasing, says that a customer came to him and wanted a Toyota Celica Liftback, but his budget would only permit him a Chevrolet Nova. The difference in sticker prices was about $2,000 with the same list of optional equipment. However, the customer was informed that because the Toyota Celica Liftback was a hot-selling car at that time, its depreciation was about 1¼%, compared to slightly more than 3% a month for the Nova. (By the way, the leasing companies figure out depreciation rates by computer, and they know what they are down to the fraction of a percentage point.) The Toyota's lower depreciation for each year increased the wholesale market value of the car. So this fellow was able to get his Toyota for just $5 more a month than the Nova, which sold new for $2,000 less.

Repossession

Even though it is unlikely that you will ever have a car repossessed, you should be aware that there are some new rules and regulations that the Federal Trade Commission has imposed on Chrysler Corporation that also have an effect on all repossessions all across the nation. Chrysler Corporation and the Chrysler Credit Corporation have come to a consent agreement with the FTC to change their repossession practices on Chrysler cars and trucks. Similar agreements have been reached with GM, Ford, and other car manufacturers over the past several years. The Chrysler arrangement, however, is the final one. From now on, this will be definitive for all repossessions. Four percent of Chrysler's dealer network, in which the parent company owns all or most of the voting stock, must pay an average of $200 in refunds to each customer whose car was repossessed since 1974. The changes will affect all future repossessions made by every Chrysler dealer; new accounting procedures extend better protection to future customers of all dealerships.

Why the changes? And why should a person who has not made his or her car payments be protected? Because the dealer can realize a profit from repossession.

Under both federal and state laws, a company that repossesses a car may keep enough of the proceeds from the resale of that car to cover the outstanding debt and the transactional expenses. Anything over that must be given to the person from whom the car was repossessed. If there is an underage, however, that person may be billed for the money the dealer has lost. Before these new rules and regulations, most auto companies had not been giving any money back, despite the profits they made on repossessed cars. There were even deals in which the repossessor, i.e., a financial institution, would sell the car back to the dealer at a price under what was owed on it. The repossessor recharged the customer for the underage, while the dealer turned around and sold the car for a profit. This is when the FTC stepped in and concluded the new agreement, and now anyone who has had a car repossessed could have money coming back if the car was sold for more than the customer owed on car payments.

Refurbishing Your Old Car

You have read about buying a new or used car, but what happens if you decide both a decent used car and an attractive new car are too expensive, yet your old car looks like it needs work? Is it worth redoing the car you have?

When you have decided that you are going to stick with your old car for a while and that the best thing to do is fix it up, the next step is to decide how much to spend and where you should put the money. Say you have a 1971, 1972, or earlier model, and it runs just fair. You can foresee a series of repairs, rust has appeared here and there, and you just don't know whether to put money into it. Before you start spending, here are some facts. If you overhaul the engine, which means a complete rebuilding, you are going to spend $500 to $600, depending on who does it. If you redo the transmission, you will spend $200, $300, or $450, again depending on who does it and how much work is done. Already you have spent about $1,000. Once you have overhauled the engine and redone the transmission, you are looking at 50,000 or 60,000 miles worth of use. Obviously, if you can get that for $1,000, you'll have your money's worth.

Peripheral items—alternator, regulator, starter, battery, and the like—can run $300 to $400. Eventually, you would have to do those items on most new cars anyway, and for almost any used car you buy you can figure on putting $200 to $300 in repairs. Figure such costs as normal maintenance expenses for any car, new, used, or "old."

Now, we come to the car's outside. If you are going to repaint it and get rid of the rust, do it right; refurbish the entire car inside and out. In studying the costs, I come up with a total figure of $2,500 to refurbish an entire old car and make it look new. It won't look like a 1979 or 1980, but if you liked it when you bought it, you ought to like it now.

Chapter 3

CAN'T AFFORD NEW? USED COULD BE THE ANSWER

How to Tell a Lemon

When it comes to choosing between a new and used car you probably ask yourself, "Why should I buy somebody else's troubles?" In many cases, you figure the former owner wouldn't have gotten rid of the car unless there was something wrong with it. Yet many people do trade cars in just for the sake of trading, and often the amount of money you save by buying that category of used car is well worth putting back into the car in order to get it in top shape. For a car to be dubbed a lemon, it doesn't need one major defect—there could be a lot of little things wrong, and the little things could be easy to fix. So don't automatically pass up an auto that seems to have some relatively minor problems if you can get the right price.

Preliminary Check What should you do to make sure you stay away from truly bad automobiles? You can tell a lot about the condition of a car without ever getting in and starting the engine. Walk around it, shove it, push it, tug it. One trip around the outside of a car can be very telling. The idea that you shouldn't kick tires may or may not be correct. What you ought to do is reach down, grasp the tire, and shake it. Looseness means defective wheel bearings, and it is probably worth staying away from the car because it hasn't been cared for properly. One of the most infallible tests of how much care a car has received and how much real use it has had is to open the door on the driver's side and see if it sags. Then don't slam it. Gently push the door closed. See whether it snaps right to, or whether it doesn't quite make it and hangs halfway open. Give it a decent push but not a slam. As you walk around the car, push down on the tops of all four fenders. This will check the operation of, shock absorbers. Worn shocks allow the car to bounce up and down several times. If it bounces once and then stops, the shocks are all right.

Remember, many things are very easily correctable. Don't count the car out yet.

Up-Close Check Points You are going to look at the tires of any used car very closely. Inspect the condition of the tread for evidence of separation or bubbles in the sidewalls. Look at those sidewalls for weathering or cracks. Cheap recaps usually show the spot where the tread joins the sidewall as a raised ridge, or sometimes a rough area. Also check the tires for wear. If the wear is uneven, there are little cuplike depressions in the rubber, and one side is worn more than the other—signs that the front wheels are either out of line or out of balance. Perhaps the shock absorbers are bad.

Always look at the ground under the engine for any trace of fluid leaks. Oil is thick and dark, steering fluid is usually red, as is automatic transmission fluid; brake fluid is clear but more slippery than water. The presence of *any* of these means you should look a little closer at this vehicle.

Grasp the tailpipe. Wiggle it, check the condition of the hanger straps. Stick your finger inside the tailpipe. Traces of oil on your finger could indicate an engine problem.

Check the trunk. What is the condition of the spare tire, and do you see the tools necessary to change tires? Make sure a jack is in there.

Always be wary of automobiles that have been in accidents. Look for any unusual ripples in the floor or signs of welding on the inside of the body panels, which can indicate that they have been replaced because of a collision.

Notice whether the windshield has little star-shaped cracks that come from the impact of stones. These eventually get bigger and will necessitate the replacement of the windshield. Look for the semicircular scratches that a bare wiper blade makes. If these scratches are severe, vision in the rain is going to be impaired. It is very expensive to get them out if you can, and if you can't it means a new windshield.

Check carefully all over the automobile for rust. Pay special attention to rocker panels under the doors and the bottoms of rear quarter panels, around the outsides of wheel openings. Rust that hasn't eaten itself all the way through reveals itself as bubbles under the paint or under vinyl tops. Look at the vinyl top, especially around the edges—little bubbles mean that it is rusting from the inside out. Stay away.

In your walk around the outside of the car, you are going to stand at one end of the car and site down the line, looking for ripples and waves in the body panels. If you see any, tap on them, listen for a sound that is more solid than the rest. That would indicate the presence of body filler. In other words, a hollow sound is fine, but a solid sound means somebody has filled it, probably with plastic or putty. Also check the spacing between the various body panels and check for a flush fit. Look for patches of paint that don't seem to match and for overspray on the gas tank and the muffler and inside the door jambs. This will indicate that the car might have been hit and certainly whether it has been repainted at all.

Looking under the Hood Now open the hood and check the fluid levels of the coolant, the oil, the transmission fluid, the power-steering fluid, and the brake fluid. A drop in any one of these fluid levels could indicate a leak or another problem. Remove the top of the air cleaner, look at the filter and ascertain the cleanliness of the inside of the carburetor. A build-up of dark sludge means the carburetor needs to be rebuilt. Check for any signs of corrosion or white powder around the battery which could indicate that it has been overcharged, that there is a problem with the voltage regulator, or that the battery itself is no good. (Check the battery for the warranty card to see just how old it is.) Check the radiator, power steering, and air-conditioning hoses for leaks. Pumps—the water pump and air pump—are driven by belts and pulleys, and if any pulley wiggles from side to side when there should not be a lot of play there, bearing wear is indicated. Also check belts for cracks or fraying.

Now start the engine. Look for signs of excessive rocking, which could be caused by bad motor mounts. Look inside the radiator filler neck after you have removed the cap, *most carefully* and preferably before the system has reached operating temperature; hunt for rust on top of the coolant tubes and signs of bubbles. Oil in the coolant could indicate a blown head gasket. Stay away from that one.

Check the fender wells and the sheet metal up around the radiator for signs of having been straightened or replaced due to a crash. Get inside the car to operate and check the function of every electrical system—radio, heater motor, interior lights, heat adjustment if electrical, and dashboard lights. Operate the heater and air conditioner, noting how long it takes for the air to heat and cool. A lengthy delay may mean that the system needs charging and that it also might be leaking.

If the car is a convertible, raise and lower the top. Hunt for rips and for cracking in the plastic rear window. Look under the rugs, if possible, for signs of rust as well as ripples in the floor pan or welding resulting from repair of crash damage. Sit in all the seats, adjust them, wiggle around in them. Feel for sagging or broken springs. Take special note of the driver's seat since this is where you will be spending most of your time, and you don't want to be uncomfortable.

Check under the dashboard. Factory wiring is usually very neatly bundled and strapped. A lot of tangled wires dangling is a sign that somebody has been under there working—and untidy workmanship on the electrical system can cause expensive problems later on.

Roll all windows up and down, open and close all the doors, and operate all the locks, making sure you have keys to fit everything. A key that doesn't fit the doors on both sides could show that a door was damaged and replaced, perhaps from a junkyard.

When you turn the key, do all the dashboard warning lights operate? All should come on with the key in the initial position, and they should go out when you start the engine. Pay attention to how long it takes for the oil-pressure warning light to go out. Too long could mean a problem.

Note whether the generator warning light flickers as the engine runs. If it does, some part of the charging system might not be operating properly. Next, turn on the headlights, and rev up the engine. A significant difference in the brightness of the lights at varying engine speeds could be the result of a problem with the voltage regulator or the battery.

Press down on the brake pedal. See how far it travels before you encounter resistance. If your foot stops close to the floor, the brake pads could need adjustment or replacement. If the pedal under pressure feels spongy, there could be air in the brake system that would need to be purged. Press down firmly on the pedal and hold it down. If the pedal slowly sinks to the floor, there could be a leak somewhere in the brake system. Now grasp the steering wheel and shake it sharply watching for excessive play, which could signify worn-out wheel bearings.

Get a Mechanic's Help   Once the used car you like has passed this self-checkout with good results, there are some tests that you might want a mechanic to perform. Besides, you will want to have a look at the car when it is up on a lift. Any good used-car dealer will let you take the car to your mechanic, although you will probably have to leave a deposit.

One of the things a mechanic can do is a compression check, a rather involved process that will give you invaluable information about the essential soundness of the inside of the engine. You are looking for consistent readings from cylinder to cylinder. A few pounds' variance in cylinder compression is acceptable, but if there is a difference in one or more cylinders and it exceeds 40 or 50 pounds, you have a problem. Diagnosis also involves squirting some motor oil down the spark-plug hole of the low-pressure cylinder. If the pressure comes up, the problem is rings; if it doesn't, the low pressure is probably caused by a burned valve.

Put the car on a lift. Look at the suspension parts to see whether any seem newer or cleaner than the others, meaning they are replacements. If you discover any such pieces, examine any area where they join the body or frame. Is anything bent or is there some kind of problem that could indicate crash damage?

Don't overlook the ball joints. They are usually distinguishable by rubber boots around them designed to hold grease. If the boots are dry or the grease on the lubricating nipple is dirty and congealed, the joints were probably not maintained as recommended and could be badly worn.

While checking around the wheels, look at the brakes for signs of fluid that could have escaped from a leaking wheel cylinder. Inspect the bottom of the differential for oil. A small drop is not significant, but more could mean a rubber seal is leaking.

Before lowering the car, examine the muffler system. Use some pliers to squeeze the exhaust pipe at various intervals along the length of the system. If it gives easily, the pipes are rotting. Then check the condition of the strap that attaches the system to the underbody. Shake the muffler, listening for rattles and noises that could mean that the whole thing is disintegrating. If everything is satisfactory, now examine the entire underside sheet metal for signs of bends, ripples, or welds. Again, keep in mind that you are looking for clues indicating damage in the past. Have a final look at the engine and transmission mounts for signs of breakage or severe deterioration of the rubber, and check the rubber lines leading to the brakes for cuts, rubs, or splits. Everything okay? Now you are ready to take a test drive.

Test Driving a Used Car

So far, you have picked at, pushed, prodded, and pumped the automobile to find out whether it is even worth taking out for a test drive. Having decided that it passes most of your tests, you are going to take it out and make it do everything a car is supposed to do. Don't just drive it around the block. Get out on the highway. Run it over a rough surface. Find a straight stretch of road where you can step on it.

The idea is to make sure you drive the car until it is well warmed up. Pay attention to the water-temperature gauge if it has one or look for the red "hot light" to start blinking at you if it uses that kind of a signal.

Engine Smoke Signals   When you first start the engine, it is good to have someone outside at the back of the car to see if it blows smoke when you first step on the gas. This could mean valve-seal problems. After you have started the engine, get out and walk around to the back yourself. If you see black exhaust, it's okay; blue smoke means engine oil is being burned. If the exhaust is blue, if possible, drive along behind while someone else drives the used car. Watch the tailpipe. If the car continues to emit that blue smoke under acceleration, the piston rings in the engine may be worn. If the smoke is blue under deceleration, as when coasting down a hill, the car could have a problem with valve guides. Both piston-ring and valve-guide jobs are expensive to fix so be careful of this.

Black smoke when you first start isn't a problem, although continuing black smoke could mean flooding, too much gasoline, a symptom that might mean an adjustment or a complete carburetor job.

While the engine is running but still cold, lift the hood, listen to the sound the engine makes. If there is anything unusual and loud like a rhythmic knock or clatter, determine the cause. Ask a mechanic if you must. Next, put the transmission in reverse, begin to back up, and listen for a clunk underneath the car during the first instant of motion. Frequently, that noise is caused by a bad U-joint or a drive-shaft problem. Also, give the car a little shot of gas, step on it a little bit. If the car jerks, squeaks, and bangs, there is a real transmission problem.

Out on the Highway   Set your speed at about 30 mph on an open road and take your hands off the wheel. If your car starts to veer one way or the other, the front end could be out of alignment. Quickly get your hands back on the wheel and wiggle it gently from side to side. Is there any excessive play before the wheel begins to turn? Yes? That's wear in the steering gear and its related components.

With the car once again at a steady speed, remove your foot from the gas pedal; then quickly get back on the pedal. Listen or feel for a thump-clunk. That will reveal any signs of looseness in the drive train.

Make both right and left turns with the steering wheel at full lock.

The turning radius should be the same length going in either direction. If not, be careful of this one. A variance could be caused by a suspension misalignment or even a bent frame.

When you reach a clear stretch of road, make some stops to test the brakes. Note whether the car stops straight in a reasonable distance. Holding the pedal down, is there a rhythmic pulsation that you can feel with your foot? A brake drum could be badly out of round or a rotor has become warped—those problems must be corrected.

Accelerate up a highway ramp or hill. Listen for engine ping. These sounds not only mean the engine needs a tune-up, but also, depending how severe it is, might mean damaged valves or piston tops.

Include in your highway test a full-throttle acceleration through all gears. If the transmission is automatic, feel for signs of slippage. If you're driving a manual, shift fast to see whether there is difficulty getting it into the gears. Whining or grinding sounds could mean worn synchronizers. With the windows up, the radio off, lift the throttle and listen for a whine in the rear end. That noise could indicate excessive wear in the rear. If the car has a clutch, note how far down you have to press before it begins to disengage, and how far off the floor it comes before it begins to engage. Too far up or down indicates the clutch needs adjustment or even replacement.

On the way back to the dealer, park on a hill, put the transmission in neutral, and set the emergency brake. The emergency ought to hold the car in place by itself. Check how close to the floor the emergency brake pedal goes. If it goes too far, you might face replacement of the rear brake shoes.

Buying Strategies That Pay Off

If you have followed all these tips, you won't have any trouble buying a reliable used car, but I still have more to tell you about the process—for instance, what *not* to do when you go out to buy a used car. Keeping these tips in mind is another way to keep from getting ripped off.

First of all, never buy a used car in the dark. Wait until you look it over in the daytime. And never buy a car in rainy weather—all cars look shiny in the rain. Make sure you have a good light day to check out your car.

Try to shop for used cars at established, reputable dealers with a fairly large inventory. Also, check to see if they offer warranties of some kind or a trial exchange period. If you are buying from a private party, your deal will be final, so be careful.

Again, no night and no rain!

Check the vehicle identification number on the registration form against that on the vehicle ID plate and the engine number if noted. Also check the sheet metal around the identification plate for signs of welding, grinding, or repainting, which can mean numbers have been switched. The worst indignity of all is to buy a nice car, get a good price, and find out later it was stolen.

Another no-no is wearing a tuxedo to buy a used car. You want to get in the car, crawl around, push around, and do all those things we have been telling you about. So, wear clothes you can afford to get a little dirty.

Never buy a car in a hurry or under stress. Never let a salesperson rush you. You have all the time in the world to buy that car. Take that time.

When the dealer's people start to put everything down on paper, don't just walk away and assume they will do the right thing. Watch everything that is written down. If the man has said he will give you a warranty, make sure he writes it down, and make sure that the price he puts down on paper is the price he quoted to you. And make sure the terms he puts on paper are the terms he quoted. Be sure he is allowing you the same amount for the trade in that he originally mentioned. *Watch the paperwork.* Never believe everything the seller *tells* you. Even if he is your Uncle John, check the car out carefully and be certain you know exactly what is happening.

Buying a Used Rental Car

What about used rental cars? Perhaps you have been told to stay away from them because they get kicked around, abused, and so on. Not necessarily so!

More and more, rental fleets are being offered to the public for sale with advertising campaigns and full-blown sales pitches, but do you want a car that has been rented to a different person every day or every week? Well, you could be getting a good buy—if you know the rules of the road regarding the sale of rental automobiles that can work in your favor.

• Number one, most rental organizations have made agreements with the Federal Trade Commission not to sell to the public any car that has suffered more than $750 worth of damage. That means that no car sold to the public has been in what could be considered a major accident.
• Number two, although a different person drives the car every day or every couple of days, not every driver is a cowboy out to kill the car.

Rental cars usually have from 15,000 to 20,000 miles on them, are generally 1 year old, and have been serviced more regularly than most privately owned automobiles. Service records almost always come with the cars so that you can see exactly what was done to them over their entire life span. These cars are generally fully equipped: almost all have air conditioning, power steering, power brakes, and many have rear-window defoggers. These features make the car worthwhile. Rental agencies know this, which is why they buy them that way.

Most rental agencies will give you a 12-month power-train warranty covering engine and transmission. The warranty doesn't cover a lot of adjustments or little things, but it will cover you in the event of big problems. Engine and transmission are where the major problems come from.

You can haggle about the price even though the agency seems to have set a figure in its ad. Most of the time, particularly because the larger cars sell very poorly, sellers can be brought down a couple of hundred dollars below their initial asking price.

Buying a rental could be a good deal. Don't automatically count the possibility out. If you find something you like, look it over carefully. See if you can make a deal.

A diesel is not the same as a gas-powered car, and buying a good used diesel takes some extra knowledge. There are special things to look for, things the prospective buyer ought to do. Although checking the outside of the car is the same as when buying a gas car, trying out the engine is different.

Try to find an owner's manual for the year and make of diesel car you are looking at. It will tell you the correct values for oil pressure, cylinder compression, and other items. Before starting the engine, give all hoses, lines, and belts a very careful check. Repeat this after running the car. Diesels have higher vibration levels, which put extra strain on these components.

Check the history of oil changes. Because of its characteristic blowby contamination, a diesel's oil requires more frequent replacement than its gas-fuel counterpart. Check to see when the owner made the changes, and you will be able to assess how well he or she has kept the car. Oil changes on most diesels should come every 3,000 to 4,000 miles or less. If the previous owner has been running more than 5,000 miles between oil changes, stay away from the car.

Use the owner's manual and follow the starting procedure to the letter, making sure the engine starts properly and sounds right. If you have never heard a diesel, listen to a good one before you go out to buy. It makes a clattering sound, which, on a car run by gas, would lead you to think the car needs valves. Not so. That is the way diesels start. But the engine should warm up and become less noisy. Listen for that. When there is no change in the sound from the moment you start it until it warms up within 5 to 10 minutes, something may be wrong. Also, the engine ought to fire promptly and run evenly on all cylinders within a few seconds. Diesel glow plugs often last the life of the engine, but a faulty injector could cause a cold spot on the glow plug, which could lead to poor self-ignition. That means one or more cylinders would not fire properly until the engine warms up. If you run into that problem, stay away from the car.

On the road, diesels are not race runners, not known for brisk performance. They are, however, highly driveable and should go without hesitation. As you accelerate, you should experience a smooth pickup, not fast but smooth and easy. If you notice jerkiness or problems in that pickup, don't buy the car.

It is also an excellent idea to follow behind the diesel while someone else drives. Follow it through a full-throttle acceleration and watch for smoke through the exhaust. Barely visible, whitish smoke is not uncommon, especially during warmup. But a heavy black smoke at full throttle is characteristic of an overrich fuel mixture, which on many diesels could mean a problem with the injection system. The injection system is probably the most expensive part of that car to maintain. If there is a faulty spray pattern or faulty injection, you will have problems. Anything more than the faintest blue smoke is indicative of abnormal oil consumption. That could be valve guides or piston rings—almost anything. Tracking the car along the highway is the most important test you are going to put the diesel through—don't forget to do it.

The Previous Owner

We've dealt with a lot of items to look for on a used car, but so far we've neglected the most important factor: the previous owner. That's because you are not always able to find out who it was. Dealers may or may not be able to tell you who owned the car before. They may not even want to if they bought it from a leasing company or a commercial fleet. If you can learn who the previous owner was, contact him or her and find out about the car.

There are two important points to remember here:

1. The old fashioned idea that low miles mean a better car is wrong. The old lady who only drove to church on Sunday is a car destroyer.
2. Flashy extras like fancy wheels, quadraphonic stereo, and racing stripes could mean the former owner was a young hot-rodder.

If this shakes some of your set ideas on buying a used car, all the better. A car that has been well cared for and properly serviced and has been on the road for long trips so that it has 40,000 or 50,000 miles on it is probably better than the little old lady's car that was used for short-trip driving.

The low-mileage auto rarely has reached peak operating temperature and therefore has never boiled out the condensation in the crank case and the exhaust system. Running almost entirely with the choke on the crankcase picks up more contaminates from gasoline. Since the engine has rarely been opened up and allowed to run on the road, there will be a carbon buildup in the cylinder heads.

What all this means is the previous owner's driving and maintenance habits are more important than the mileage.

Effective Bargaining

You have made your selection, you are in love with this used car—now comes pricing. How do you haggle for a car?

When you buy a new or used car, remember that the first price asked is rarely the price the seller actually wants. If you pay it, you have probably overpaid by several hundred dollars.

Above all, haggling requires psychology. When you reach the stage of talking money, keep in mind: (1) you want to pay as little as possible; (2) the seller wants to sell the car for as much as possible; and (3) cash is the name of the game.

• Be prepared to act quickly to get the deal you want. Don't have to walk away and borrow the money from Uncle John. Make sure Uncle John is with you when you make the final deal.
• Put the seller on the defensive without being insulting.
• Don't appear to have too much money in your pocket. As I told you before, dress casually and don't drive up in a brand-new car, even if it belongs to Uncle John.
• Be prepared to walk away from the whole deal. Remember: it takes a lot of nerve to make a low offer and stick by it. The seller may not accept immediately but he or she could call you back if a better offer doesn't come along.
• Don't get too emotionally involved with your car. We know you'll fall in love with the car, but don't do so to the point where you pay the first price automatically.

- When a car is advertised as "make an offer," never make the first bid. Force the seller to tell you what price range he or she is looking for. Dealers know how much pressure there is to sell that car, so even when things seem to be going your way, don't give in too quickly.
- Let the seller think that you are paying your absolute highest price.
- Offer some choices—for instance, ask the seller to fix some items, to accept a trade, or to throw in extra equipment. Make those choices less attractive than a low-dollar cash offer. (Many of the things you ask for you could probably do yourself.)
- Give the impression that you are looking at other cars. Make the seller think that if he or she doesn't act quickly you will buy something else. Should you reach an impasse, take another look at the car, act as if you are mulling over your decision. Time is on your side, but don't leave without giving the seller one more chance to make you one more deal.
- Find out as much as possible about why the car has to be sold. The quicker a car must be sold, the lower the price you will have to pay.

One final word on buying any car, new or used, from a dealer. Never sign anything that is not completely filled out with the proper figures and that does not spell out everything you are supposed to get. If you have been promised new tires at no cost, make sure the sales slip shows this. Make sure the word "new" is down on paper as well as whether they are supposed to be radials or another special type of tire. If you have been promised that something will be fixed, be sure the seller spells it out for you. The words "check" or "inspect" do not mean "fix." Insist that everything is written out, right down to an oil change with new oil filter. The term "tune-up" does not mean that you will get new plugs or points or anything else unless every detail is in black and white.

Although you may not have convinced the seller to give you all the improvements you want, at least you have what you've agreed upon in writing. If you discover you have been cheated, you have the proof on paper.

Chapter 4

THE WARRANTY
STORY

What a Warranty Does

Let's look at the warranty on your new car. It covers you in case you get stuck with a lemon—or does it? Well, at least it covers whatever goes wrong—or does it?

You expect every new car to have some kind of warranty to cover all those little things that are going to go wrong in the first few thousand miles. Every car has some kind of problem—requiring perhaps a simple adjustment, perhaps real work—and you want to be sure that the warranty covers whatever work you need.

Warranties have been confusing folks for years. All that fancy language just didn't make a lot of sense until a recent law, the Magnuson-Moss Warranty Act, cut through most of the gibberish and made understanding a little easier. The law now says that warranties have to be written in ordinary language, and every term and condition should be spelled out. The warranty is a written guarantee by the manufacturer that it will stand behind the car. A **full warranty** says that all defective parts will be fixed or replaced free of charge, is good for anyone who owns the product during the warranty period, and states that repairs will not require unreasonable efforts by the consumer. In other words, they can't ask you to drive your car back to Detroit. If the product can't be fixed within a reasonable time, you are entitled to a new one, or your money back. A **limited warranty,** however, eliminates some of those guarantees. For instance, it may cover parts but not labor, or impose other conditions.

Verbal promises and published advertising can serve as warranties, but you are much better off getting something in writing, preferably on the bill of sale. Then, as far as the laws of the land are concerned, you are in good shape. Your complaints ought to be handled without your resorting to the courts.

Obviously, the most important part of buying an automobile is making sure of the backing of the dealer and the manufacturer. Buying from a reputable dealer is the first step in avoiding future problems. If possible, talk to people who have purchased from a particular dealer to find out if that dealer stands behind his cars and service department. Start by calling the local Better Business Bureau. Find out about the frequency of complaints against particular dealers, and, as I say, if you can talk to their customers, all the better. You can also assume that dealers who have been in business for a long time are generally concerned about repeat business. They may go that extra step to keep you happy so that you will come back and buy your next car from them. Unfortunately, today many dealerships have changed hands six and seven times over the past few years, and it can be very difficult to find the ones that have been around for a long time. If you know of one, try to do business there.

The Extended Warranty

This is the era of the extended warranty, and it pays to know what to look for and whether it's worth your while to put out money for an extended warranty. I do not know of any automobile without some kind of extended warranty package—some you pay for, some are free.

GM was the first manufacturer to make a ripple in the warranty program. They extended the coverage on the power train in cars and light trucks beyond the 12,000-mile limit to 24 months or 24,000 miles. This new service benefit is called Power Protection Plus, or PPP. It extends the warranty on major engine parts (gas or diesel), the transmission, front- and rear-drive axle components, and the drive train in general. All work performed before the regular 12-month, 12,000-mile limited warranty continues to be fully covered. Customers pay a $100 deductible for any power train repairs required between the 12,000- and 24,000-mile mark or 12- and 24-month mark.

Ford was next to move into the warranty coverage. They include a similar $100 deductible, 24-month, 24,000-mile protection plan for all cars and light trucks except the Lincoln Town Car and the Continental Mark VI. The warranty on the Lincoln Town Car and Continental Mark VI has been extended to include, at no extra cost, the coverage provided by this Ford extended-service plan, called ESP. You now have EPP (Extended Protection Plan) and ESP. Since Lincoln already had a 24-month plan last year that you paid extra for, adding the ESP to it means that the Lincoln Town Car and Continental Mark VI are now warranted through 36 months or 36,000 miles. (Chrysler also announced a similar warranty coverage for its cars and light trucks except for the Imperial.) Are the extended warranties worthwhile when *you* have to pay for them? To help you decide, here's an overview of the warranty plans American manufacturers have developed.

I mentioned the Ford ESP, which costs a $100 deductible when work has to be done on the major power-train components. ESP also provides limited car rental and towing assistance from the first day of ownership if the vehicle is held overnight for repairs and requires towing to the dealer. ESP was introduced by Ford in the fall of 1976 and is a sale item. The customer actually pays for it. It will continue to be a sale-item option on some models, although Ford is offering it for nothing on others.

GM offers an optional extended-service package called the Continuous Protection Plan. It offers optional power-train protection for 36 months or 36,000 miles and 5 years and 50,000 miles. This *you* pay for.

American Motors and Chrysler also offer buyers of new cars extra-cost, optional extended-service contracts. The AMC program, called Service Security Plan, or SSP, extends major-component coverage to 36 months or 36,000 miles. Chrysler's package covers the power train for 5 years or 50,000 miles. Chrysler's new Imperial carries a special comprehensive 24-month/30,000-mile warranty that covers everything but tires. It also includes no charge for maintenance, which means free oil changes and free everything else in the way of maintenance right up to the 24-month/30,000-mile period.

Actually, whether it is a factory plan or some other kind, every automobile dealer offers some type of extended-service plan. Most cost from $150 to $350 and offer you power-train warranties—for the engine, transmission, and rear end. If you have problems with them, you pay only a deductible of $50 or $100 on any work that has to be done.

Is it worth paying that money for an extended-service plan on a new car? Do you feel you expect to have work costing $150 to $350 on that car (remember the deductible of $50 or $100)? The answer depends on what you require for peace of mind. Generally, today's cars do not need major servicing after the 12-month period but may before the 24-month period. GM has had problems with its transmission, but the company has been fixing these kinks whether or not you had the extended-service plan. When it comes to an item that gives every customer problems, the manufacturers fix them without charge.

But suppose something else goes wrong. How much will repair cost over and above the deductible plus the cost of the service plan? It is very doubtful that you will have any real problems with your car that will cost more than $450. Therefore, spending $350 for a service plan plus a $100 deductible may not be the wisest move. On the other hand, if a service plan costs only $150, it might be a good buy because it is quite possible to surpass $250 on needed repairs during the warranty period.

If you opt for an extended warranty, get a service plan backed by a major company. Do not pay good money for coverage from an unknown insurer.

If you can do your own work or have a mechanic you trust, forget the policy altogether. And if you trade in a car every 2 years, do a lot of traveling, or move from city to city, don't bother with extended warranties. They won't meet your particular needs.

Again, used-car warranties are only as good as the dealer who sells the car to you. The longer the warranty, the higher the price you will pay for the car, and the more the warranty covers, the higher the price you will pay. These practices are only common sense from the dealer's point of view, and it's up to you to decide (1) whether you want to pay extra for a better warranty, and (2) whether the dealer can be trusted to stand behind the warranty after you have paid for it. Dealers don't say to you, "This warranty costs X number of dollars." They quote a price included on a used car with the warranty. If you can do your repairs or are sure the car is sound, you can bargain down the price by making it clear that you are not interested in the warranty.

Lemonaid

Preventive Medicine   What do you do when you end up with an automobile that just doesn't want to work right? For, despite the fact that most automobiles today come off the line in pretty good shape, the lemon does exist. For years automotive engineers in Detroit and other places have been claiming that there is no such thing as a lemon, that any car can be fixed. It is just not so. Every single year, 20 million automobiles are built on planet Earth, and you know that there are bound to be flaws, and sometimes unfixable flaws, in some of them. Unfortunately, it may be you who gets one of these lemons.

Let's begin this unpleasant subject by exploring ways to avoid getting a lemon. The point to prevention is not to accept any car until you are sure it is as good as it can be when you drive it off the dealer's lot.

• You should inspect any new car. You should check it out *before* you take delivery. You have a warranty, and the salesperson will always say to you, "Well, if there is anything wrong, we will take it back and take care of it." That's fine, but things you can see on the car or find on the car before you leave the dealership, should be taken care of *before* you accept your car.

• Never accept delivery at night. See your car in the daylight, drive it around the block at least once, check the interior and exterior for dents, scrapes, nicks, rips, etc.

• Make sure that all the fluid levels under the hood are correct, make sure the car is absolutely ready to go, and when you drive around the block, listen for noise—squeaks, rattles, vibrations while the car is idling, anything that sounds a little wrong.

• If you discover something, bring it to the attention of the salesperson or the dealer, and don't accept the car until the problem has been corrected. I know you want your new car right away, but you are much better off waiting an extra day or two to get it in perfect condition.

Keeping Records   We mentioned that you certainly should check out your car carefully before you even leave the lot with it. For the first few weeks and months that you own the car, treat it as though you were a critic paid to discover every flaw. Keep a pad and pencil handy; note every little twitch, every rattle, every possible sign of trouble. Catalog every symptom by date and mileage. If you find something wrong, let the dealer know. Go on record as having registered a complaint. If you bring that car in for service, make sure you receive *and* keep a copy of the service ticket and that it states exactly what you have asked to be fixed.

Try to establish an ongoing relationship with someone at the dealership, whether it be the service manager, the salesperson you dealt with, or the owner, if you can. Make sure they are aware each time you are in for repairs and what the problem is. List the time and date of all calls to the dealership, the nature of your complaint, the name of the person you spoke with and what he or she recommended to be done. Sounds like you suddenly became a bookkeeper, doesn't it? But if you ever have to go to court over this automobile, you want to be able to show just how much of a nuisance it has been to you. Documentation is very important when you are trying to win a court case.

Registering Complaints   Your car has been causing you problems, you have been to the dealer, who hasn't come up with an answer, and you just don't know what to do. First, go to another dealer. You are under no obligation to have your car serviced by the place that sold it to you. Your warranty must be honored by any authorized dealer of the kind of car that you bought, although you might be treated to an argument. For example, the second dealer might tell you that your job will go last in line.

If the dealer does such a thing, however, take the complaint directly to the manufacturer. There is a number you can call, usually toll-free, listed in your owner's manual. Each auto manufacturer has a system to process and handle complaints. If you contact the manufacturer's customer-service representative in your zone (each manufacturer divides the country into special zones), this person will investigate your complaint and work through the dealer to correct it. Manufacturers have been attempting to improve their performance in the service area, but problems remain. There are also consumer boards across the country, and the Better Business Bureau is working with some manufacturers to help resolve consumer complaints. In addition, the National Automobile Dealers Association is setting up arbitration panels through local dealers' associations. Located in many parts of the country, these panels function more or less in the same way. You come in, and they arbitrate your case against a particular dealership or against your particular car and decide for or against you. Still unsatisfied? If so, it could be time to take your case to state and local authorities. Almost all states have some form of consumer bureau, and many cities have them. And of course, you can complain to appropriate national consumer groups.

In the eyes of the U. S. Government, a lemon is a lemon only if it presents a safety problem. When there is a flaw in enough cars of the same type, they can be recalled for correction. Supposedly, recalls are ordered by the manufacturer, yet most come about as a result of consumer complaints and federal government mandates. If you believe your car has something inherently wrong that makes it unsafe to any degree, describe the problem in a letter and fire it off to: Office of Defect Investigation, NES 30, 400 7th Street S.W., Washington, D.C. 20590. You can also call the toll-free National Highway Traffic Safety Administration Auto Safety Hotline by dialing 800-424-9393. Ralph Nader's Center for Auto Safety also keeps files on lemons, and has prompted recalls in certain instances.

The Center's address is 1223 Du Pont Circle Bldg., Washington, D.C. 20036.

Court—the Last Resort

Suppose you have tried all the above-mentioned means to solving your car's problems and still have a lemon that by now you would like to dump. At this point, you can take your case to the courts, which have been responding very favorably to lemon cases. First, you are going to need a lawyer. Second, you will face legal fees, although the Magnuson-Moss Act says that an at-fault company is responsible for paying legal fees. Indeed, if you win the case, the court can order this to happen, and there is also a good chance your lawyer will be paid by the company.

Many people don't go into court with lemon cases because they think the required legal fees are going to be as much as, or more than, they are going to get back on their defective automobile. Not necessarily so. Court can be well worthwhile if you have kept records, are able to show that the car has been out of your hands for repair many times, and that the whole business has been bothersome. It is quite possible that you will win your case in court and that the company will refund your money or offer you a new car. This has been happening all over the country and will continue to happen.

For instance, the case of Ventura vs. Ford involved a 1978 Mercury Marquis that was bought for about $7,800 from Marino Auto Sales in Plainfield, N.J. After eight trips to the dealer to cure a stalling problem, Mr. Ventura took Ford to court in January of 1979. Ventura's lawyer, Mark Silver, accepted the case with just a $350 retainer. The lawyer then won, and Mr. Ventura got $7,000 back— the original purchase price minus 9¢ for each of the 8,000 miles he had driven the car. Having won a favorable decision, Mr. Silver asked the judge to award his $5,165 fee. And he got it. Obviously, Mr. Ventura wouldn't have gotten much back had he had to pay that attorney's fee. But the court ruled that, under the Magnuson-Moss Act, Ford had to pay the attorney.

How important is this case to you? Well, it means that now, with Ventura vs. Ford as a precedent, any court could be willing to have attorney's fees taken from the company, assuming you win your case. And, even more importantly, eight trips back to the dealer is really a small number of trips to call the car a lemon. The decision indicates that many courts are becoming tougher on manufacturers. If the dealer or manufacturer does not solve your problem for you, if you are without your car for too long, if you have a problem that could be a safety hazard—as in Mr. Ventura's stalling on the highway—get your money back or go to court.

From this point on, I'm assuming that you have bought your car and intend to get the most out of it. So, I'll start with the ins and outs of good gas mileage and go on to ways of taking care of your car for the next 100,000 miles. Much of what I have to say is common sense, and much can be found in the owner's manual, which so many people neglect. There will also be some ideas that you may never have heard before—some that might even scare you—like running water through the carburetor. All of the procedures we will consider together are tested and proven. And you can try them out safely for yourself. In my collection of cars, I have several in use every day that have over 100,000 miles on them. Getting the most out of a car isn't hard to do with proper preventive maintenance, careful driving, and common sense.

ON THE ROAD

Chapter 5

BETTER MILEAGE— MYTH & REALITY

You can hear the cry in every barroom and living room. And entire families have needed outside intervention when the subject of the gasoline shortage has come up. Somebody says there are cars that run on propane or natural gas. Then there is always somebody who invariably brings up the Fish carburetor, or his cousin's best friend's mailman's sister from Pittsburgh, who went all the way to Florida on a tank of gas in a Lincoln Continental. Or the other biggie, the guy who puts a pill and water in a gas tank, and the car runs.

Let's separate a little fact from fiction if we can. The story of the magic carburetor varies from claims that there was a man named Fish who sold it to Ford who has it hidden in a basement to rumors about an Italian invention that has been bought up by the oil companies and kept off the market so that the oil giants can sell more gas.

First, no carburetor or other fuel system can take a full-size car from Pittsburgh to Florida on a tank of gas, so forget that. If a Mr. Fish ever invented anything, it was probably cod liver oil. This story jumps out of the woodwork once every five years, and, inevitably, somebody believes it and passes it on. The reason that the magic carburetor is not on the market, according to the tale tellers, is that the oil companies have paid off Ford, Chrysler, GM, or somebody else to keep it under wraps. Phooey! My friend, if Ford, Chrysler, or

GM had a miraculous carburetor, they would have it on the market so fast it would take your breath away. This would be true under any circumstances, and particularly now, when the car companies are straining to meet the federal fuel-economy standards, which get tougher each year. Remember that the auto makers may sip cocktails together at the Brook Cadillac in Detroit, but when they go back to the plant they are out to sell cars, and they will cut each other's throats without a qualm. If one manufacturer possessed some kind of a wonder carburetor, they would inundate the airwaves, newspapers, and magazines with stories and commercials to tell the world about their discovery.

And the guy with the pill? Well, if you bought his pills and put water in your tank, you just proved that P. T. Barnum was right again. The most important thing to remember about cars and fuel is that a certain amount of energy is necessary to move a certain amount of weight a certain distance. Add to this the speed you want to move at, think about Newton's laws along with Murphy's laws, and you realize there is no silver bullet coming down the pike to answer the energy crisis. No Masked Man is going to ride out of the sunset to solve our energy problems by gunning down the villains.

Gasohol

Gasoline and alcohol do mix, as long as the mixing is done in your fuel tank. The argument over alcohol as a fuel for cars has been going on, not just for the last couple of years, but since an internal-combustion engine was first attached to wheels as a means of locomotion. Back in 1895, the inventor of the modern internal-combustion engine, Theodore Otto (didn't know that, did you?), recommended alcohol as a fuel for his 4-stroke motor.

The engine in your car, by the way, is a 4-stroke or 4-cycle engine. In many foreign countries, alcohol has been used mixed with gasoline and, in Germany in World War II, by itself as a fuel. In the U.S., an alcohol fuel called "argole" was sold in service stations throughout the Midwest.

Why then all the questions about alcohol today? The fact of the matter is that alcohol has been more expensive than gasoline up until now, and even at present in this country, alcohol costs more to make than gasoline. But look out, those OPEC fellows are rapidly causing the price of gas to reach that of alcohol!

Some of the experts say that one reason why alcohol is so expensive is that it has been made in large quantities only for drinking purposes, and plans to make a lower grade that would still be a good fuel-quality alcohol could turn out the stuff much more cheaply. Put simply, wasting good drinking alcohol in your car would be a sin, but automobile-grade alcohol could be made and actually would be cheaper than gasoline at its present prices.

To use pure alcohol would present some problems, though. Without going into all the chemistry, a gallon of alcohol produces about 50% less power than a gallon of gasoline. The figure for ethanol is somewhat better than for methanol, and that's why, when some experts talk about alcohol, they are actually talking about ethanol. Ethanol is generally made from wheat, corn, barley, and the like, leaving a residue for animal consumption, whereas methanol is produced naturally by the decay of garbage and can be produced in other ways, including from coal. Using pure ethanol, Brazilian experimenters have recorded a mileage *decrease* of about 15% to 20%, while experiments with methanol show about a 50% mileage decrease. Very simply, these alcohols really are not replacements for gasoline. Strangely enough, however, adding 10% to 15% ethanol or methanol to gasoline results in a mileage increase. The process is all very complicated, but what it amounts to is that the addition of alcohol to gasoline increases the octane rating of gasoline. The combination of ethanol and gasoline has proved to be the best because it doesn't separate out as badly at low temperatures as methanol does. Also, the mixture burns cooler and cleaner and allows some spark-timing advance to give better mileage—which means that there is gasohol in your future.

Careful, though! Some rubber and plastic components in your fuel system could suffer deterioration from the alcohol.

In some places, gasohol is available as an unleaded fuel; elsewhere, as a leaded gasoline; and, in a few places, both ways. Be careful if your car calls for unleaded. You can use gasohol, but only unleaded. If your car uses leaded gas, the addition of alcohol gives it even a better boost. A regular gasoline before lead is added might have an 81 to 84 octane. After lead is added, it is probably 86 to 89, and, after ethanol is added, the octane can go up as high as 92 or 93. You can get a better octane with an alcohol mix of 10% with gasoline, but not more than 10%. Today's cars are not made to run on more, and more than 10% will cause problems in some cars. Whether your car uses leaded or unleaded fuel, you are going to find it running cooler and better on gasohol, which will also knock out the knock and ping.

Should you buy gasohol? There is no evidence that says gasohol is bad for your car, but you need to check one thing before using gasohol. *Make sure your fuel filter is metal.* A plastic filter will not hold up under alcohol. Some cars still use the plastic fuel filter, but you can easily replace it with a metal one for a couple of dollars. Other than that, gasohol will not cause any problems as long as you stick to the 10% alcohol mix sold at most pumps. Which means that if you make your own, shoot for 10%, too.

You can expect to change fuel filters a couple of times soon after you switch to gasohol. Alcohol tends to clean out your gas tank, taking with it dirt and sludge. That's fine, but be sure to clean the fuel filter and replace it after the first few tanks of gasohol.

Gas-Saving Devices—Do They Work?

Almost everywhere you look today, someone is trying to sell you something to save you gasoline. For a while, the federal government stayed out of it, and only the automotive and consumer magazines did any testing of these devices. Now, the Environmental Protection Agency has jumped into the fray. The federal agency has tested many of these items. Their verdict? Most do nothing, and the few that actually do save gas cost more than they save.

The so-called gas savers fall into several categories and we will look them over one at a time. (By the way, there is one type that does save fuel but breaks the law by interfering with the air-pollution devices on the car. This kind is available and some people use it, but it must be removed when the car goes for its state inspection.)

First, let's look at gasoline additives. The EPA says to forget them. Most are just petroleum derivatives and distillates or alcohol.

They do nothing. Some may have a detergent that cleans the carburetor, so if your carburetor was jammed with dirt you might see some improvement, but a good carburetor cleaner would do just as well and probably far more cheaply.

Then there are devices that bleed air into the carburetor. These are useless if your carburetor is properly set up. One device that blocks the EGR (exhaust gas recirculation) valve and bleeds air in can save gas, but that is one of the illegal types for a mechanic to put on. You would have to put it on yourself.

Devices that attach to the ignition are also useless. If your car is properly timed, it is going to give you all the mileage it can. (We will be thinking more about that later.) Devices that tie into the fuel line—magic vapors, ion tubes, or magnetic pulsars, or whatever they are being called this week—are equally useless.

This brings us to the value of timing.

Fact: The one way to get the best mileage from your car is to have it properly tuned. Once you are sure the plugs are good and the carburetor is properly adjusted, the timing can be advanced to a point just before the engine starts pinging. Realistically, a 4- or 5-point advance is the most that should be made. Further advance can bring about other problems.

All in all, both the EPA and the independent testers have come up with the same results—no magic gas-savers, no secret potions. The only real gas savers are a proper tune-up and good driving habits.

Popular Phonies   All the experts agree that fuel-saving devices are fake, but that doesn't stop the hustlers. The gas shortage and the high cost of gasoline are bringing all the thieves out of the woodwork, and magical devices like the so-called Pogge carburetor, the Fish carburetor, and the wondrous Italian carburetor are all back. I am going to give you just a few items advertised in a very popular magazine. In their classified-ad section, you find come-ons like: "Miracle carburetor, 100 miles per gallon. Drawings for $10"; "Water injection systems, $5"; "Cut your gasoline bill. 10 ways to improve your gasoline mileage, $2." And how about this—"Save hundreds of dollars on gas, oil, and engine repairs. Get the details free!"

But the "free details" are going to tell you how to spend money, believe me.

Other ads exhort you to enjoy auto air conditioning without wasting gas; to convert your car so that it will run on wood for $12.50; or to get a ring and valve job *while you drive* for just $6.75! Incredible. Well, there's no shortage of phony gas savers out there, including the Pogge carburetor, which has apparently been getting a real reaction because the Post Office Department inspectors called me to ask me about it. I hadn't heard of it for years. The people selling this so-called automotive miracle say that for $50 they will send you the plans for a carburetor that will get 25 miles out of a pint of gasoline. Okay, send them the $50, and kiss it good-bye, friend, because there ain't no such animal.

Fact: The most important part of saving gasoline is *you,* the person behind the wheel. You will save gasoline with your driving habits.

Water Injectors   Unfortunately, some products that actually could be of use to the modern motorist have been ignored in the rush to throw millions of dollars away on gas-worry cures. One of these is the water injector. Some fly-by-night outfits have claimed that water injectors hooked to the car's vacuum system could increase mileage. They have sold these things, which are no more than a plastic bottle and some rubber tubing, at prices from $20 to $50, and the people who bought them wound up with nothing. As a result of this fraud, real electronic water injectors that might have done something for today's cars were passed up because they were more expensive and required expertise to install.

A little background is in order here. Water injectors have been around for many years in one form or another, but the most recent heavy use of water for the internal-combustion engine was during World War II. The U.S. Air Force had to get heavy bombers with a full load of bombs and fuel off short landing strips in the Pacific. The problem was getting the huge engines to spin at a tremendous rate of speed quickly, without overheating and flying to pieces. The solution was to carry several thousand gallons of water, which were injected with the fuel at take-off and when the bombers had to make a fast exit from a bombing target after releasing explosives. The water cooled the engines sufficiently to accomplish what was necessary. The water did not stretch the fuel supply by any great margin, yet, when called upon, it allowed added power without causing the engine to disintegrate.

What application does this have today? Simply this: The same effect of more power without the strain can be gained in automobile engines with water injection. It helps cars suffering from ping. Ping, detonation, preignition—call it what you want—it's that sound like marbles rattling under the hood when you strain up a hill or accelerate hard when entering an expressway. The conditions are the same, in miniature, that the big bombers were faced with: the need for quick power strains today's car engines and low-test gasolines.

If this is true, why not use the vacuum-operated, cheapie type of water injectors? The answer is simple. Modern cars develop maximum vacuum at idle. That vacuum drops as the car accelerates. In other words, a vacuum-operated water injector gives the most water when it's least needed and vice versa. The electronically controlled water injector, however, is set up to deliver the maximum water supply on demand when the engine is called on to work the hardest. These units sell for anywhere from $60 to $140, depending on the make and the supplier, and unless you are a pretty fair shade-tree mechanic, on top of this outlay you will probably have to pay to have them installed by someone who knows what he or she is doing.

By the way, if you do decide to add an electronic water-injection system to the old buggy, you might put a 50-50 mix of alcohol and water in the reservoir. This will give the same cooling effect and actually add a little boost to the power. It might also save a little gas. The saving, however, would probably not be enough to compensate for the cost of the injection unit and the alcohol, unless you keep the car for some time. The injector also might allow you to advance the timing without ping, again increasing mileage.

A Half Hour to Better Mileage

Actually, better mileage is more a matter of how your car is and how you are than of anything you could add to the car, subtract from the car, or accomplish with fancy gimmicks. If your car is tuned properly, your carburetor clean, your timing set-up, and if your tires are properly inflated, your car will give you the best mileage it possibly can, assuming that you don't put your foot through the floor so far that you have to roll up your trousers. You yourself are 90% of the mileage you will obtain from your gallon of gasoline. And there are some immediate measures that you can take to make your car better even if you are not trained to do tune-ups and don't like to get your hands dirty. They are easy to do and the salesperson at your auto-parts store can help you with what you need and how to go about doing them.

1. You can replace the air filter.
2. You can replace several other filters on today's cars that do clog up. You can take care of the fuel filter, just in front of the carburetor, yourself. It's very easy to put on.
3. You can put certain additives in the gas tank just to get rid of the water pumped in from one of the service stations you stopped at that didn't have clean tanks.
4. On some cars, you can even turn the top of the air cleaner over so that you get a little more air into the carburetor a little more easily. And that, too, will increase your mileage a little bit.

Treasures from the Auto-Parts Store

You can also buy some items that might save you a few miles per gallon, but they can be expensive. Consequently, the same folks who a few years ago were running out for fancy carburetors and manifolds and wonderful things to make cars go faster are now running out for the same items to obtain better mileage. Strangely enough, they are not asking for the impossible. Auto manufacturers do a good job of making cars as economical as possible. After all, the federal government has those corporate average fuel economy, or CAFE, regulations, and they demand that auto manufacturers meet a certain mile-per-gallon average on all cars. Government standards have been powerful motivations, and now the driving public is demanding improved fuel economy even faster.

Although the aftermarket, i.e., auto-parts stores, has no miracles for sale, there are a lot of devices that can make an improvement in your fuel economy. The gadgets run the gamut from simple attachments to complicated contraptions that look as if they were invented for the Apollo space program. Some devices try to make up for shortcomings in the car's original design, others gain fuel economy at the sacrifice of some other aspect of the automobile's performance.

Perhaps the most basic economy accessory is simply a **stiffer throttle spring.** If the standard spring on your car is too weak, your foot causes the throttle to move with every irregularity in the road, and every time the throttle opens, the accelerator pump shoots an extra, unneeded squirt of gas into the engine. A stiffer spring can be an important part of your economy package.

Electric cooling fans will have an effect on fuel economy. That is why they are becoming standard on high-mileage cars. Many foreign cars have had them for years, and American cars are now including them.

Don't assume that replacing a catalytic converter with a plain piece of pipe will result in more miles per gallon. The new converters are getting very good reduced emissions while not restricting exhaust flow much more than a regular muffler does. The early converters tended to lump up inside and give problems, but the new ones hold up well. Removing yours is not going to give you any better mileage.

The same applies to replacement carburetors. Some older standard carburetors are so heavily burdened with poorly designed, troublesome emission hardware that stripping everything off and bolting on an unfettered high-mileage aftermarket carburetor can transform a car. But if your car runs decently and gets reasonably good mileage, it is not likely that a replacement carburetor will make any significant gain.

A change of gearing often yields more mileage. Consider replacing a 4-speed transmission with an overdrive 5-speed, new or from a junkyard. Or install a lower numerical final-drive ratio. Up to a point, lowering engine rpm's to obtain the same speed lowers fuel consumption as well as internal wear.

Turbocharging has become a big word, one of those words everyone likes to hear. For a while nothing but engine breakers, turbochargers have improved and can give you a slightly better miles-per-gallon average, although basically they are not miracles.

Most of the gas saving you realize is based on replacing a large, heavy, standard engine with a lighter turbocharged unit, producing the same power with less weight to carry around, which means that the mileage has to go up. Simply adding a turbo to a car does not guarantee more miles per gallon. Assuming that you are a moderate driver and that you drive the same with a turbocharger as you did without it, you may get better mileage. Unfortunately, most people who put a turbocharger on a car immediately go out and *use* it—use it as if the car were suddenly a hot rod, wasting gas in the process.

Tip: the cost factors on most of these items negate the gas savings unless the car is kept for many, many miles.

Mileage and the Diesel Car

If you know anyone who owns a diesel car, either one of the American models or an imported job, you will hear him or her crow about great mileage and the lower price paid for diesel fuel. There are some things a diesel owner does not talk about, however. Like diesel clatter, the smell, and the problem of finding a gas station that sells diesel gasoline.

And besides all that, there is the wait for the glow plug to warm up before starting the car, and the crawl of acceleration, particularly when trying to pass. Passing at 60 mph on a 2-lane highway could turn out to be more suspenseful than an Alfred Hitchcock thriller.

Very few people are aware of one other item—a 42-gallon barrel of crude oil supplies only about 8 gallons of diesel fuel. That same barrel of oil will supply 18 gallons of gasoline. Obviously, the rest of the barrel is used for other products after the 8 gallons of diesel are refined out, but the other by-products are not the ones in short supply—the gasoline is. Because diesels only get about 25% higher mileage, they really do not help the fuel shortage. In fact, if all cars were diesels, we would be in more serious trouble than we now are. Indeed, if more and more diesels hit the road, their drivers are going to see higher prices, simply because of supply and demand.

If all this is true, why has Detroit suddenly begun producing so many diesel cars? The answer is simple. Each manufacturer must meet certain federal fuel-economy standards. The corporate average fuel economy figures, or CAFE figures, are obtained by averaging the figures of all cars sold by the company every year. By making all its big cars—Cadillacs, Oldsmobiles, and others—get over 20 miles per gallon as diesels, GM improves its overall fuel-economy figures and does not have to depend on massive sales of the smaller cars to meet federal regulations.

Now, if you own a diesel, a few tips.

• Be sure the diesel fuel you buy is matched to the weather in your area of the country. Additives are available in most auto-parts stores that prevent diesel fuel from thickening in cold weather, but properly weatherized fuel from the pump already has an additive. The problem is that some service stations do not sell enough diesel fuel for you to be sure that they will have winter grade in their tank when the first cold weather hits. For this reason, the additives are a good buy unless you are absolutely sure of what you are getting at the pump. The risk you take is sludging up your entire fuel system and having to be towed to the dealer for an expensive clean-out job.

• Using No. 2 fuel oil from your home-heating tank can get you slapped with a heavy fine. It is not as pure as fuel refined specifically for your diesel. We always recommend that you follow the manufacturer's maintenance program on any car, and with diesels, that is imperative.

• Change the oil filter at specified intervals or you will be flirting with real problems. An add-on fuel-filter separator is a good buy to prevent water from fouling the engine, a common occurrence with diesel fuel.

The GM Diesel   I am going to spend some more time on the subject of diesels, particularly General Motors diesels, which have been doing so well in the market but not so well mechanically.

The GM diesel is really a converted gas engine that has not proved itself as a long-life engine. If you own a GM diesel, one piece of aftermarket equipment that should be put on immediately is a water-separator filter. It costs about $50. Not only has GM decided that this is a good idea, but recently they have also added another piece of electronic equipment to their diesel-powered passenger cars—an electronic water-sensor system, designed to warn when excessive water is in the fuel tank. Placed in the tank, it has a provision for siphoning out water without the need to remove the tank from the vehicle. These units are installed on the production line and also offered by the dealers in a $50 kit. Anyone who owns a GM diesel vehicle should get one.

GM continues to believe that the best protection owners can have would be the assurance that the water content of the diesel fuel sold at service stations is within the stringent limits set by a number of states. The problem is, not all states set limits. And not only that. Even within those states where limits are set, they are not checked often enough. Diesel fuel does collect water, and it does gum up the engine and the injectors. If you get too much water through that engine, you are faced with a job and a half . . . at a price and a half.

GM passenger-car diesels have come up with a 25% better fuel economy over the gas engines, but they have not come up with the reputation for reliability that diesel trucks and Mercedes Benz diesels have gained. Despite GM's claims, durability is not one of the features you receive when you buy the Olds diesel or any of the others. The biggest seller among GM diesels, the Olds, had camshaft problems and then a string of other problems. GM played down these reports, but a Los Angeles market-research company, J. D. Power & Associates went out and did some surveys. They learned that 78% of Olds diesel owners in the survey experienced engine problems with their automobiles. GM did go beyond the normal 12-month/12,000-mile warranty in fixing many diesel engines, yet the 1978 and 1979 cars had accumulated more miles than the warranty allowed, and GM is trying to make owners pay for these engine repairs.

Some people have not had properly running diesels from the very beginning. Others have been plagued by constant water fouling because there was no special separator.

An old issue of *Consumer Reports* magazine raps the Olds diesel. When researchers put 49,000 miles on a 1979 Delta 88 diesel, it averaged a little more than 21 miles per gallon and used a quart of oil every 2,600 miles. That's the good news. Maintenance and repairs, they say, are the bad news. This year, according to *Consumer Reports,* they spent $650 on routine service, oil-filter changes, and so forth, while mechanical repairs on the diesel engine came to $880. Those repairs included fixing oil leaks, replacing rocker arms in the left bank of the V-8, installing an engine oil pump (the second one), and a big item, $525 to replace the fuel-injection pump, a problem many diesel owners have run into.

Owners' comments on a *Consumer Reports* questionnaire as well as letters from readers indicate that the researchers' problems with their car were not unique, that the GM diesels are just not holding up. GM says all the bugs have been ironed out. I hope that they will do something for the people who bought the earlier models.

The 55-mph Speed Limit

Now let's have a look at the law that everybody hates, the 55-mph speed limit. I want you to imagine yourself walking down the street in a 55-mph wind. You would almost be knocked over. That wind is, in effect, what your car must cut through at maximum legal speed. It's what holds your car back, and what takes up gasoline. And every increment of speed is the same as increasing the wind by that much, slowing your car down that much, and using up a proportionately increased amount of gasoline. Actually, any speed over 35 mph brings into play this air-resistance factor, which causes your car to burn gasoline less efficiently. Therefore, a 55-mph speed has significance for your mileage.

And since getting good mileage is the name of the game you want to play, here's a tip that won't cost you a cent. If you are accelerating on the highway and then suddenly take your foot off the gas in order to maintain a steady speed once you've reached the maximum, you are using too much gas. It is much better to start backing off the gas pedal when you hit 50 mph, so that by the time you hit 55 mph your foot is where it is going to stay. You actually save gasoline that way.

Tip: Keep the windows closed. Open windows cause air resistance that costs you mileage. The loss is more than the loss from using the air conditioner with the windows closed!

Chapter 6

KEEPING YOUR CAR ONE STEP AHEAD OF THE JUNKYARD

Your Owner's Manual

I would like to encourage you to do some reading in addition to this book. What I have in mind is a book that many people ignore although it can save the life of their cars. Some researchers found out that more than half the people they talked to totally ignored the owner's manual that came with their automobile, and yet that manual provides the knowledge they need to keep their cars running for 100,000 miles or more. Still, nobody seems to want to read it.

Good maintenance, of course, is the key to any automobile's life, and the maintenance for your car is outlined in the owner's manual. Read it, and pay attention to it. You will learn every maintenance item with the mileage at which it should be checked. What are the important maintenance jobs that manual is going to tell you about?

It directs you to ascertain the fluid levels in radiator, crankcase, transmission, brakes, power steering, and battery. It says when to change the oil and oil filter. It tells you to check the drive belts, water hoses, and battery charge; to flush and refill the radiator and to inspect the brake linings; to inspect the tires and check the pressure; and to change the automatic transmission fluid.

Most importantly, the owner's manual states that your driving pattern will govern when these checks should be done. The idea that you have to go 3,000, 6,000, or 12,000 miles before you check something is not really correct. Owner's manuals recommend more frequent changing of motor oil and transmission fluid for vehicles in severe service, which could apply to your car. I am not talking about driving in a desert, I am talking about stop-and-go driving in the city, in both hot and cold weather. This kind of use is the toughest way to put miles on your car, and it is considered "severe service."

The owner's manual is not trying to sell service: you can do a lot of the maintenance yourself. The owner's manual is trying to get you to take care of your car and obtain better mileage from it.

How Your Car Works

What happens when you turn the key in your auto? The starter motor cranks the engine, which moves the pistons inside the cylinders. The motion of the pistons brings in a mixture of air and gas. At that point, the ignition system, by means of the spark plugs, puts a spark to this mixture, and the engine starts running. The combustion of the fuel/air mixture inside the cylinder forces the piston down. Then, the process starts all over again.

The up-and-down motion turns a crankshaft, which, in turn, turns the wheels at the back of your car. Although rather simplified, this is a lot more than many people know about what happens when they set their cars in motion. The biggest point in what I just described is that fuel must enter the cylinders for anything to happen. Fuel is what burns and causes the pistons to go up and down. You have a fuel pump that draws gas from the tank into the fuel line. Next the fuel goes through a filter to prevent dirt and dust and then heads for the carburetor or, in some cases, the fuel injectors. The carburetor or injectors mix the fuel with the necessary amount of air to enable proper combustion. If too much gas enters the cylinders during cranking, the engine will flood and die. If there is too much air, the engine burns too hot, too lean, because it doesn't have enough gas for optimal burning.

The explosions in the cylinders that cause the piston to go up and down require more than simply dumping in gas and air. As I've already said, gas and air have to be mixed in the correct proportion.

The camshaft opens what is known as the intake valve. As the piston comes down, the fuel/air mixture is drawn into the cylinder through that valve. As the piston moves back up inside the cylinder, the intake valve closes, and the fuel/air mixture is compressed into a very small area at the upper end of the cylinder where the spark plug is. The spark plug sparks, ignites the mixture, and the resulting explosion forces the piston back down.

What happens to exhaust? There are piston rings on the piston that form a seal to prevent a leakage of those expanding gases. When the fuel/air mixture burns and becomes exhaust, the camshaft opens the exhaust valve. The piston then moves up a second time, forcing the waste products from the explosion through the exhaust valve and out the muffler and tailpipe.

A weak spark that sometimes fails to ignite the mixture causes missing, loss of power, and pocr fuel economy for your car. You also pollute excessively if you have a misfire. Missing can cause that popping noise in the exhaust. These are indications that you need a tune-up.

Let's review the process once more but from the perspective of what is known as a 4-stroke engine. The first stroke is downward, pulling in the fuel/air mixture. The second stroke is upward, compressing the fuel/air mixture until it explodes when ignited by the spark plug. The third is the down, or power, stroke that actually drives the car, and the fourth stroke forces the exhaust through your muffler and tailpipe. Fuel combustion is the main ingredient in driving your car. But electricity causes that fuel to explode, thanks to a spark from your spark plug. Electricity comes from your battery. Your battery is 12 volts, so because a spark plug needs over 20,000 volts you have a coil. I won't get into the electronics of it, but the coil takes the 12 volts and multiplies it to the 20,000 needed to fire off that spark plug cleanly. The electricity goes from the coil to the distributor, which acts like a card dealer in passing out current to each spark plug. When you look into your engine compartment you will see the distributor. It is the helmet-shaped item that has wires running to the spark plugs. It will have four, six, or eight wires, depending on whether your car has four, six, or eight cylinders. If you should hear a metallic rattling, a knock or ping as you accelerate, go up a hill, or put heavy pressure on the car, your plugs are probably firing too soon. If your car runs sluggishly, and you are getting poor fuel economy, it could mean that they are firing too late. In either case, you want the timing checked. A timing check is part of a standard tune-up. On today's cars, most carburetors can't be touched, and almost all the tuning of the car is done with the timing.

I said that the coil takes 12 volts from the battery and multiplies it up to 20,000 volts. If that was all that happened, the battery would not last very long. You might get a mile or two and then find the battery dead. While the engine is running, the battery is constantly recharged by the alternator, which is driven by a fan belt coming off the motor. A car engine *almost* entails perpetual motion. The motor drives an alternator that sends electricity to recharge the battery, which sends sparks to the plugs to run the motor. A perfect circle, so to speak. To make sure the battery isn't damaged by overcharging, the voltage regulator monitors and adjust the alternator's output. You will have a light on your dashboard (some cars still use gauges, but most cars have "idiot lights") that says "alt" or "gen," abbreviations for "alternator" or "generator." If that light stays on while you are driving, something is wrong with that charging system. It could be a bad alternator, a loose or broken fan belt, a faulty voltage regulator, or perhaps a loose or disconnected wire. You ought to have the problem checked out before you wind up stranded on the road with a dead battery.

Once the engine is in motion, your spark plugs are sparking, the fuel is igniting, and the car is rolling—or is it? It is if your transmission is functioning properly. The transmission is what comes between the engine and the wheels. It is what takes power from the crankshaft of the engine back to the wheels and gives you motion.

Your transmission has several different gears. The faster the engine turns, the more power it can make. The lower gears allow the engine to turn faster for the extra power needed to accelerate from a stop, or to climb a steep hill. A high gear lets the engine slow itself down for longer life and better fuel economy yet still gives enough power for highway speeds. A manual transmission means you shift the gears from low to high, and an automatic transmission does all the shifting for you, automatically. You should check the fluid level in an automatic transmission periodically because it is the fluid that causes the pressure that gets those gears to change and gets the car moving.

Your car also has what is known as a differential. As you go around a curve, the differential lets the outside wheel turn faster than the inside wheel because the outside wheel has farther to go. The differential won't drive both wheels if one wheel slips. When you are stuck in sand or mud, you have to put something under your tire to make sure you get traction. Or gently apply the parking brake and the gas at the same time. That will make the differential work for you.

In order to stop a car, you step on the brake pedal. When doing that, you send hydraulic fluid through thin brake lines to the wheels. The pressure of the fluid forces the brake shoes against the wheel drums in the rear and the disc pads against the front-wheel discs. The consequent friction slows the car and finally stops it. Eventually, friction wears brakes out, so they should be checked regularly. If the brake warning light comes on when applying the brakes, you might be low on fluid, you might have air bubbles in the brake lines, or the hydraulic cylinders could be worn. Have them checked.

What about steering? When you turn the steering wheel, it turns gears inside the steering-gear box, the steering gears move rods connected to the front wheels, turning the car.

Automatic Transmissions

Most American cars still have automatic shift even though somewhat of a changeover toward manual transmissions has begun. People feel that for city driving the automatic is the way to go. No shifting, ramming, running, and jumping all over a gearshift lever while in traffic. On most automatic transmissions, you have two low gears in addition to a drive gear. You have a second, or L2, for use in heavy traffic. Although most people disregard it, it is also recommended for descending medium grades to avoid riding the brakes all the time, which could cause overheating of the brakes.

Second gear makes the engine run faster and use more gas, so using the brakes instead, if they are needed only once or twice to slow down, could save you money in the long run. The first gear, L1 or low on the selector, is for hard pulling through snow and mud or climbing steep grades. For fuel economy on a downhill slope, you might be tempted to shift into neutral and coast, but neutral gives you no control over your car, is illegal in many states, *and* is unsafe. If the engine should die while idling in neutral, the steering wheel could lock, the car would be moving at high speed, and you would have no control at all. Coasting could increase the load on the brakes and damage the transmission.

After you park a car with automatic transmission, you shift into park and apply the parking brake, which relieves the load on the transmission, particularly if you happen to be on a hill. Of course, always shut the engine off when you leave the car. That way you eliminate this business of a car that supposedly pops from park into reverse and takes off. Shut the engine off, put on the emergency brake, take the strain off the transmission. The transmission may last a little longer, and the car won't run backward after you as you walk away.

Taking Care of an Automatic   Automatic transmissions are much more susceptible to damage than manual transmissions. Yes, the guy with a heavy foot on the clutch, the person who rams that gearshift, can tear up a manual pretty easily. The automatic, because you don't do much shifting with it, tends to be forgotten, and problems come because you start treating it more roughly than it deserves or can handle.

• You should not run up the engine high for more than 10 seconds while holding the vehicle with the brakes. You've seen people who like to dig out at the stoplight and beat the car next to them. They rev up the engine while holding the vehicle back with the brakes, tearing the transmission to pieces in the process. You get the same effect when you run the engine up to high speed while the transmission is in drive and the driving wheels are stuck in snow or sand or against a fixed barrier. The wheel starts spinning at a tremendous rate, the transmission overheats, and you are in trouble.

• Rocking a car out of the snow by keeping it in drive and rocking backward and forward, taking your foot on and off the gas, is fine. What you *don't* want to do is let the stuck wheel spin for more than 10 or 15 seconds—that could wreck your transmission. Rock if you must, but when you reach the peak of the forward motion, get off the gas.

• Don't shift into reverse while the car is moving forward. That, too, tears up a transmission. When backing out the driveway, it is easy to forget and use the transmission to stop the car and start it forward by shifting from reverse to forward. Don't do it. Stop the car with the brakes first, then shift into the proper gear.

• Keeping the car motionless on an upgrade by accelerating the engine instead of applying the brakes is another sure way to kill a transmission.

• Avoid parking for a prolonged period with the engine idling and the transmission in gear. Shift into neutral, and put the emergency brake on, or shift to park. Don't sit with your foot on the brake, the engine in gear and idling. Don't shift into park while the wheels are still turning. The few people who do this find out very soon that it is the wrong way to handle an automatic transmission.

• Don't shift out of neutral when the engine is running at high speed. This is something people do without realizing it. For example, the engine is idling too high because it was set too high by a mechanic, and you bang into first gear or reverse. When going into drive or reverse from neutral, there should be just the slightest feeling of catching. If the transmission slams hard and you feel it in the seat of your pants, your foot is too far down into the gas pedal or the engine is set up idling too high. High idling can occur when the choke is on during the first moments after you have started your car. That is normal; however, the transmission still should not hit too hard when it engages.

Tune-ups Some auto-repair shops have a service referred to as a transmission tune-up, which includes straining the fluid and installing a new filter and gasket and new fluid. It costs $20 to $25, and sometimes there are specials on the service. If you are tempted, hold on—there is one thing to watch out for. Some places that advertise specials are doing so to get you in the door with your transmission.

Once they have the pan off, they will show you the metal filings, and tell you, "Look at that. Your transmission is chewed up!" Unless you have been having a problem, forget it. Metal filings are normal in the pan. In fact, the pan is actually there to catch those metal filings. They are part of the breaking-in process in any transmission and can be found in any car that has run 1,000 miles or more.

Fluid Checks What about changing transmission fluid? Some companies say you don't ever have to change the fluid, others say change it every 100,000 miles. This is all a matter of opinion, but I change fluid at 15,000 or less on any car. It is inexpensive enough to have that done and save the life of your transmission.

If you have been rocking your car in sand or snow, hauling heavy loads, or doing prolonged idling in stop-and-go traffic, especially in warm weather, have the transmission fluid checked. If the fluid is discolored, has a burned smell to it, internal parts such as transmission bands or clutches may have overheated. Immediately changing the fluid and the filter and screen can prevent further damage that might make an overhaul necessary.

All manufacturers advise routine inspection of the fluid level every 5,000 to 7,000 miles. However, the owner's manual may say something like this: "Under severe or abnormal driving conditions, the fluid and filter should be changed at approximately 15,000 to 24,000 miles." To manufacturers, "severe" means frequent trailer pulling, heavy stop-and-go driving, particularly in hot climates, and driving in snow or very cold weather. The suggestion is for most people to get that fluid drained and changed and the screen or filter cleaned at least before 30,000 miles. (I say between 15,000 and 30,000 miles; the auto companies say between 15,000 and 25,000. Make your choice, but get it done to keep your transmission alive.) Even on models for which fluid changes are routinely recommended, the service could be needed more frequently than normally advised in the owner's manual. Most manuals suggest a change at 20,000, 25,000, or 30,000 miles. If you do it at 15,000 miles—what I routinely recommend—you eliminate problems caused by dirty fluid. Transmission fluid is highly detergent, and one of its uses is to keep all those finely meshed parts clean. Once the fluid gets dirty, it no longer does that job, and you begin to have dirt acting on your transmission.

Tip: Perhaps you have not had the transmission fluid changed for 50,000, 60,000, or 70,000 miles. You went by the owner's manual, and it said you didn't have to change it. Should you get it changed now? Yes and no. Yes, take the car in, have the pan dropped, the filter or screen taken out and cleaned, and the entire transmission checked. But *no,* do not let them throw away the old fluid, unless it is so badly burned that it is useless. If it is still red at all, save it and filter it, even if you use a handkerchief, and put the old back in, adding only as much new fluid as needed. Remember: Transmission fluid is highly detergent, and putting fresh fluid in a car that has not had new fluid for 50,000 or more miles will clean off all the varnish buildup. And by this time, your transmission is running on that varnish buildup! You don't want to lose it.

One of the areas I usually stay away from is advising what kind of auto transmission fluid to use. There are several types on the market—Dexron, ATF, and so on—and your manual will call for a specific kind of fluid. If you can find it, good. Use it. But note this: Most auto-transmission repair shops buy their fluid in 55-gallon drums. They use the same fluid from the same drum for every transmission that comes in. In the early life of a transmission, the differences in these fluids may have an effect, but, later on, once the transmission has become gummed up with varnish and everything else, the type of fluid used is not as important as making sure you have good fluid.

I get arguments on that, particularly from the people who make the special types of fluid. All I can say is that it is rare to walk into a transmission repair shop and find more than one kind of fluid. Usually, they use a decent name brand from a large drum and put it in everyone's car.

Manual Transmissions

More and more cars are being sold with manual transmissions because they improve fuel economy from 8% to 10% on some models. If you own a manual, keep in mind that low, or first, gear uses 30% more fuel than second. For minimum maintenance and maximum economy, shift from low to high as fast as you can. Don't exceed the speed limit recommended for each gear in the owner's manual. That is the only way you get that gas saving.

Sensible Shifting After you have driven the car for a while, you will know when to shift just by listening. If the car has a tachometer, the dial that shows how fast the engine is turning over, you can shift precisely right at the recommended rpm's. Beyond that, there are several shifting do's and don't's that can preserve your transmission and save gas.

• You will reduce wear if you hit the clutch pedal fully whenever you use it and keep your hand off the shift lever while driving. Never ride with your foot on the clutch, and never race the engine as you let out the clutch.
• Many people never remove their hand from the shift lever. Perhaps they think it makes them look like Mario Andretti, not realizing that when Andretti has his hand on the shift, he is on a racetrack and is shifting ten times to the mile on a 500-mile course. *You* don't drive that way.
• If you stop at a light for more than 30 seconds, put that transmission in neutral, and take your foot off the clutch to avoid overheating.
• As the car slows down when you apply the brakes, you may have to downshift two or more gear positions, from fourth to second, in order to prevent lugging. Reduce speed for a stop by taking your foot off the accelerator or by using the brake, not by shifting into lower gear to slow the car. That puts unnecessary wear on the clutch and, again, you are not racing.
• In normal city traffic, don't downshift for braking purposes on a slippery pavement. That can cause a momentary loss of steering control with a front-wheel-drive car or fishtailing with a rear-wheel-drive car.
• The only time to downshift is in mountainous areas, where it may be better to downshift on steep grades than to put wear and tear on the brakes.

Long-term Maintenance Always be sure the clutch pedal has enough play so that it moves down a half inch to an inch, depending on the car, before the clutch engages, and that it requires more pressure to push it to the floor. Adjust your clutch if the amount of play exceeds that. If a clutch pedal goes too long without adjustments, it will begin to slip, and the engine will race as if it were in neutral. Eventually, the clutch will have to be replaced, and on today's cars that is an expensive job. Other signs of clutch wear are shuttering or chattering or jerking when you let out the pedal.

Fluid levels in both the transmission and differential should be checked with each oil change or when you notice erratic or notchy gear shifting. Both are signs that the level is low. On most cars, manual transmission lubricant does not require changing but can need some adding to if it gets low.

On front-wheel-drive cars, a single unit called a transaxle incorporates both the transmission and differential. Usually in the rear axle in rear-wheel-drive cars, the differential transfers engine power to driving wheels and allows the front and rear axles to turn at different speeds when you go around a corner. It also makes the wheels spin when in snow or ice. It is an important part of the car because without it you would jerk and bump when you turn.

If you don't like that spinning action you get in snow or sand, when you buy a new car get one with a posi-traction rear end or posi-traction transaxle. When one wheel starts to spin, the other will still grab. Posi-traction is expensive and hard to repair. Service for the transaxle is similar to that of the two elements—transmission and differential—of the rear drive car, and any good mechanic can handle it. It should be checked and serviced.

Chapter 7

REPAIRING YOUR DREAM CAR

How much of your money on auto repairs actually pays for auto repairs, and how much lines the pockets of a mechanic who is ignorant and/or trying to rip you off? The fact is that 53¢ out of each dollar spent on auto repairs is wasted. This is according to a survey released by the U. S. Department of Transportation in May 1979.

Finding a Good Mechanic

With all that waste, how do you find a mechanic who will do the proper job? How do you find a mechanic who will guarantee the work? How do you find a mechanic who will do only the work that needs to be done? These are two of the questions I am asked most often. I never personally recommend a mechanic because the one I recommend will get 99 out of 100 jobs right, and the person I send will be the one who is botched, so I turn out to be a dummy. Not wanting to look like a dummy, I do not recommend mechanics. However, I can help you find one, or at least keep you from getting ripped off.

There are some maintenance jobs that you as the consumer should do for yourself as well as many that your mechanic will have to do for you because of the Code of Responsible Automotive Services Practices. Oh yes, there is such a thing, and it includes several guidelines, with the main goal being customer satisfaction. Mechanics who subscribe to the code recommend only those services necessary for vehicle safety, performance, comfort, and convenience, explaining to the customer which services are required to correct existing problems and which are for preventive maintenance. They offer the customer a price estimate for work to be performed, obtain prior authorization for all work done (in writing or by other means satisfactory to the customer), and notify the customer if appointments or completion promises cannot be kept. They furnish an itemized invoice of fair prices for parts and services that clearly identifies any used or remanufactured part, and furnish or post any warranties covering parts or services, permitting customer inspection upon request of replaced parts. They also maintain customer-service records for a year or more, exercise reasonable care for the customer's property while the car is being serviced, maintain a system ensuring fair settlement of the customer's complaints, and cooperate with established consumer-complaint mediation activities. The Code of Responsible Automotive Servicing Practices provides some tips as to *what* you should look for in dealing with any mechanic.

Now, here's *how* to find that top-quality garage or mechanic.

• *Word of Mouth*—The best way to find a mechanic is through the experiences of others. Yet this is not the easiest kind of information to get since most people are in the same predicament as you are, and most people do not even know when they have a good or bad mechanic. Since most car repairs could be performed by your little brother in the back yard, most mechanics get away with murder— until they hit something difficult, something a little hard to find, or something a little hard to fix. That is when they destroy your car.
• *Certified list*—A directory of garages that employ certified mechanics is published by the National Institute for Automotive Service Excellence, 1825 K Street N.W., Washington, D.C. 20006. The problem with the directory, however, is that there are many good mechanics out there who do not have time to take the test for

certification or really do not care because certification has not become as widespread as it possibly should be. You could be missing a lot of good mechanics by sticking to the so-called certification list.
• *"Environmental surveys"*—Look at the mechanic's environment—the shop and the quality and condition of the equipment in it. This is a good measure of a mechanic's potential although not proof of knowledge. A clean shop is wonderful. It means that the people there have clean habits, that when they work on your car they will probably be clean. But it's still not necessarily proof that your car will get fixed properly.
• *Prerepair diagnosis*—A good mechanic is a good diagnostician and should be able to give you more than a generalized idea in plain language of what is wrong with your car *and* put it in writing. The estimate should be detailed and include the cost of parts and labor. If you are left with any doubt, shop around. Get several estimates. Auto repair is a competitive business, and prices can vary. Have each mechanic tell you what will be done for the price. If one says your brakes can be repaired for $40, another says $80, and a third says $120, the question is, Can you get away with the $40 job, or do you need the $80 or $120 job? It is easy to put shoes or pads on a car, much more difficult and expensive if you actually work on the brakes—grind down the drums, hone the cylinders, or even replace wheel cylinders. Find out what needs to be done.
• *Price*—How can you be sure you are not overcharged? Comparison is the best strategy, but there are other ways. There are flat-rate manuals listing the amount of time a particular job should take and all the parts that will be necessary. These could help you establish a ballpark figure for the work in question, but be aware of the controversy about the worth of the flat-rate method. Critics charge that some of the repairs are overestimated in the flat-rate books, and measuring strictly by the time involved leads to hasty, often insufficient, repairs. Still the flat-rate charge defines a price range, and if you look at one of these manuals, you may come up with some prices that will give you a general idea. Realize too, though, that a shop with mechanics working a flat rate does not take into consideration problems that may arise in a tough job or the fact that sometimes a job can be done much more quickly.

Many times the automobile owner brings on his or her own

problems with a mechanic and then blames the mechanic when the problem is not fixed. Let me give you an instance. The car is chugging, bucking, fighting you. You drive up to the mechanic's shop and you say, "There's something wrong with the carburetor. Can you fix it?" And the mechanic says, "Sure, I can." He repairs it, but it turns out that the carburetor was not causing the problem. It may have been the ignition, or a vacuum line, or any number of other things. The mechanic, you see, followed *your* instructions. When you drive the car out, and it is still bucking and kicking, you conclude that the mechanic is terrible. It's your fault. When you went to the mechanic, you should have described the symptoms and said, "Check the car out and fix what's wrong, but call me first to tell me how much it's going to cost." In a situation where diagnosis is necessary, the mechanic may not be able to give you that written estimate ahead of time. Having done the diagnosis, which will certainly cost some money, the mechanic can then call you and tell you what the total job will be. And by using proper diagnostic techniques, the real problem will be worked on.

On-the-Road Repairs

When you are far from home and stuck, you cannot really get comparison figures. One answer to this dilemma is to join a reputable auto club. Many at least pick up the cost of getting you to a mechanic and generally have on their rolls a mechanic they trust. To avoid committing yourself to really expensive repairs, try to do whatever it takes to get your car running. Ask for itemized bills and a breakdown of parts costs and get permanent repairs after you return home. Do not get a valve job in the middle of Keokuk, Iowa, when you do not know anybody in Keokuk, Iowa. Do not let anyone put in a new drive shaft in Pocatello, Idaho, if you are just driving through. Have the repairs made that are absolutely necessary, get the car running, and take it home.

Beware of mechanics who find problems with your car that are not obvious to you while you are driving. They will tell you about worn shocks, unsafe tires, leaky radiators, misaligned front ends, and/or other parts you ought to fix before they get worse. Take their advice—when you get home. Do not give a stranger a big job. Have someone you trust check it out.

Be wary of "preventive maintenance" offered when you are away from home, particularly on the road. Let's face it, some guy in the middle of the roadway, out of nowhere, making money off passing vehicles and tourists is not someone who worries whether you will come back angry.

The best policy is to have your car thoroughly checked before leaving for a trip and have on board the tools and parts necessary to fix disabling, but not serious, problems such as a broken fan belt, flat tires, and blown fuses. Do not leave home with flat spares and no jack.

Dealing with Your Mechanic

You have finally found a mechanic you think you can trust, you are satisfied with the work the person has done in the past, and now you are going to get some new work done. How do you make the thing go smoother? How do you make sure your car is going to go in and out with everyone concerned knowing what is supposed to happen so that the repairs turn out just the way you want them to?

Well, first of all, try to call for an appointment. I understand that you cannot predict emergencies, but for normal repairs, call for that appointment. Why? Because there are about 100 million cars on the road and only about 800,000 mechanics. It is much better if you have an appointment, and better yet if you can request work on Tuesday, Wednesday, or Thursday, that is, a day in the middle of the week. Most people decide to bring their car in on Monday or Friday. Monday, because they had trouble on the weekend and Friday because they would like it fixed in time for their days off. When you can schedule your appointment for the middle of the week, the mechanic has the proper amount of time to do the job, and chances are you'll be paying for a much better job. Arrange ahead of time just how long the shop will need the car, and try to allow as much time as possible not only to repair the car, but also to road test it to make sure the job was done properly. Do not stand over the mechanic's shoulder because you have to hurry to work. Try to plan

103

for some alternative means of transportation when the car is in the shop.

By the way, when choosing your mechanic, try to find a shop that is close to public transportation. Ask whether the shop provides a loaner car. Some places do, though very few. There is nothing more annoying than sitting in a mechanic's waiting room for several hours.

If you are not satisfied with the way the work was done once you have your car back, register your complaint immediately. Do it right there with the people who did the work. Do not go somewhere else to have the mistake corrected and then go back to the original mechanic expecting your money back. Life just does not work that way. You complain to the person who did the work. If you are not satisfied, if you cannot reach an agreement, go to a Better Business Bureau, consumer action panel, or other consumer-protection group for help.

Tune-ups

What is a tune-up? From time to time, every car gets tuned up. What exactly does that mean? What will a tune-up on your car do for you? What won't one do for you? A lot of people expect a total rattletrap to go in for a tune-up and come out sounding like a new Cadillac. That just does not happen.

Will a tune-up give you better gas mileage? Possibly. If your mileage has been dropping, a tune-up might restore some of the mileage you had before. Do not expect a car with poor mileage to improve just because you have it tuned up. If the car had poor mileage the day it came out of the factory, tuning it up is not going to make much difference. If you happen to own a 1973, 1974, or 1975 car without a catalytic converter, the mileage will be poor from the start. Catalytic converters allowed the auto companies to remove a great deal of the air-pollution junk that was causing poor mileage during the years 1973–1975.

Will a tune-up make the car peppier? Will you get more spunk, zing? Usually it will, assuming you have no other major mechanical problems. Your car's performance does depend heavily on the tune-up, but remember: If the car was sluggish when you bought it, tuning it up may or may not make any difference. Sluggish performance can be dangerous, so make sure your car is tuned properly. And if the sluggishness does not disappear, check other things like valves and rings.

Symptoms   How can you determine when your car needs a tune-up? One of the first things to do is to keep a running check on your gasoline mileage. If you know your average mileage for three tankfuls, when the average drops by over 15%, chances are you need the engine adjustments known as a tune-up, and maybe some other work, too. Other symptoms of an out-of-tune engine are:

- idling too fast when the car is warm
- stalling
- low power
- rough idling
- knocking or pinging
- hard starting, misfiring, hesitation, or rough running
- the engine running with the key off
- black exhaust smoke

If you can mentally check off a number of these problems with your car, the remaining question is, How much will it cost? It is not very expensive to have your car tuned up. Many of these symptoms require minor adjustments. A federal government survey showed that most problems resulting in low gas mileage and poor running of cars were caused by spark plugs or minor malfunctions. For example, a common problem is the idle speed: too low, the car can stall; too high, the engine continues to run even after the key is turned off. Often a mechanic can adjust the idle speed quickly with very simple tools and a couple of dollars' worth in parts. Ignition timing is another typical problem. This is often the culprit when you experience hard starting, pinging under acceleration, or loss of power. Like the idle speed, ignition timing is often adjusted inexpensively.

You want to ask the mechanic to check the engine before replacing anything. If a few minor adjustments can do the job, there is no reason for you to pay for a lot of unnecessary parts. If your engine is running well once those adjustments are made, forget major parts replacements, but keep a constant check, making sure the idle and ignition are okay. A bad case of pinging can literally cause your engine to disintegrate over a period of time.

There are simple repair manuals for almost every car model available. You can find them at bookstores or auto repair shops. Whether you do your own repairs or not, it's a good idea to get one and read it over.

How Often? I have had conversations with people who boast, "I have been driving for 60,000 miles and never changed a plug." I am willing to believe anything I am told; I am very gullible in that respect. But this kind of claim is hard to believe. If I were asked whether someone should run as long as possible without a tune-up, my answer would be no. Even when your car exhibits none of the symptoms I mentioned, you should have it tuned periodically as specified in the owner's manual. Generally, with today's hot ignitions, we are talking about every 12 months or 12,000 miles if you use leaded gasoline, and every 24 months or 24,000 miles if you use unleaded. A tune-up is a good investment. You can prevent the kinds of problems that eventually cost a lot of money, help keep your mileage where it should be, and keep your car from breaking down on the highway, which is one thing everyone wants to avoid.

How Thorough a Job? The next question asked is, "Can't I just change the points and plugs?" No. Changing the points and plugs is only one aspect. A thorough tune-up is a complete process consisting of at least four steps:

1. Check cylinder compression to determine whether a mechanical problem exists that a simple tune-up would not help.
2. Check the full ignition system and the carburetion and pollution systems against the specifications set down by the manufacturer. Usually, these are on an underhood decal. Otherwise go to the owner's manual.
3. Engine-idle speed, ignition timing, vacuum, mechanical advance, points dwell, plugs, condenser, distributor cap, rotor, ignition coil, spark-plug wires, PCV system—all of these need to be checked with engine-testing equipment. The PCV and air filters, battery and automatic choke, and vacuum hoses can be checked visually.

4. All filters should be changed regularly, even between tune-ups. They get dirty and can harm the engine. Check them visually, change them regularly.

An item that a lot of mechanics forget and might need a reminder about from you is that it is always best to spray clean the carburetor before beginning the adjustments. There is no point in adjusting a dirty carburetor. Spray clean it first, then see whether it needs some adjusting.

After the tune-up has been completed, whether you or a mechanic is doing it, road test the car to make sure it runs well. Do not just drive the car from the mechanic's garage to your home. Drive it around. If it is not reacting properly, if you have sputtering or any kind of a problem, get it back to the shop immediately. Do not let the mechanic have the opportunity to say, "Well, something you did in the last three days caused this." Get it back as soon as you realize it is not running exactly the way you want it to.

Cost   What should a tune-up cost? Some garages have signs out front saying a tune-up costs X number of dollars for X number of cylinders. Be advised that nobody knows right off the bat what a tune-up is going to cost unless the mechanic does the same work on every car that comes in the door. And if that's the case, you cannot be sure that you are getting a proper tune-up or that you are not paying for parts you do not really need. You will probably be getting the equivalent of a check-up. When you talk to someone about having your car tuned up, check the cost if it needs only adjustments and check what it will cost for the full job, including replacement of parts. Do not let any work be done that has not been specified and agreed to.

Do-It-Yourself Tune-ups   Surveys show that more than a third of the tune-ups done today are performed by the car owners themselves. They may not do the whole process, but at least they can do most of it. With a few dollars' worth of equipment and a good automotive tune-up manual specifically for one's type of car, almost anyone who can handle a screwdriver, a pair of pliers, or any other common tool can do a tune-up. Many of today's cars have sealed systems, which means there are only certain procedures that you can do anyway. Why pay someone $40 or $50 to do something you could do in your backyard in a half hour with parts that cost about $15?

What about Rebuilt Parts?

There is much talk about whether you should rebuild carburetors, alternators, and starters, or replace defective parts with brand-new ones. Obviously, cost is a consideration, although the biggest problem is that both rebuilt and new parts come out of the factory or rebuilder just as bad as they went in. I quote to you from a letter from Ralph's Garage in Springfield, Massachusetts, to *Motor Age* magazine. On the subject of using rebuilt parts, Ralph writes, "I have seen many times when I have had to replace as many as four or five rebuilt starters on one car before I could get a good one. I have tried six different rebuilders—in my estimation rebuilt parts are about as good as a hound dog that can't smell a pail of onions."

Ralph says he now does all his own rebuilding. He does not necessarily buy new parts but does his own rebuilding. Many mechanics, garages, and service stations do their own rebuilding and stand behind their work. If they must use a rebuilt part from an outside source, most will check it carefully.

It is your job as a consumer always to make sure that you have the proper guarantee on any part that is rebuilt or comes rebuilt from another company. The slip on the repair order should state the length of the guarantee, usually 30, 60, or 90 days. But remember, just because the mechanic puts something in your car—whether it be an alternator, carburetor, or starter—does not mean that the part is a good one. As much bad junk comes down the line in manufacturer's boxes as comes down the line from cars that have been run 100,000 miles. So, if you are still having problems with your car after a repair, don't hesitate to suspect that whatever has been put into it was (poorly) rebuilt.

Wheel and Tire Care

Wheel Alignment   One of the biggest items people are being ripped off on is quickie wheel alignments. What should you look for in a wheel alignment? Some places that are more interested in selling you a new set of tires than getting your car to run properly will point out how badly your wheels are out of alignment by showing you how terrible your tires look. They will sell you the tires, do a fast adjustment on the wheels, and off you go to wear out another set of tires.

The great problem with having cars aligned today is that few mechanics and fewer drivers really understand what the job should include. Too often, a so-called wheel alignment is no more than quick adjustment to eliminate a steering pull to one side and doesn't include the essential checking and correcting of the basic angles of the wheel.

A proper wheel alignment begins with a careful examination of the tire tread. The difference in distance between the front and rear of the tires on the same axle, if misadjusted, will cause a peculiar sawtooth or feather-edge development on the tire treads. This is called the "toe." Your tire may have to toe in, toe out, or go straight ahead. A good wheel-alignment shop will have all the specifications for your car on toe as well as on camber. The camber angle is the inward or outward tilt of the wheel. If it is incorrect, wear shows up on the inner or outer two treads of the tire, while the rest of the treads remain normal. A combination of incorrect angles causes more complicated wear patterns. You may indeed need new tires.

Before attempting to correct any wheel-alignment problem, a mechanic should check the entire front steering system for excessive wear in the ball joints, tie rods, idler arms, inner-shaft bushings, and look for loose wheel bearings and sagged springs. Overlooking any of these will render the wheel alignment inaccurate and a complete waste of time and money. Don't let someone align your wheels when there is excessive wear in any of the steering parts. The alignment will go right out again.

Once the steering system has been carefully checked for wear and is tight, the alignment begins. A thorough job has to include adjusting to specification the toe, the caster angles, the camber angles, and the steering wheel position. The steering wheel has to be centered when the car goes straight ahead or the car isn't aligned properly. An alignment should also include a check of the steering access inclination and the turning radius. These technical terms might not mean much to you, but a good alignment mechanic will know what you are talking about and will check these things.

Tire Pressure   Wear can also be caused by tire inflation. Overinflation causes premature wear of the center treads. With underinflation, the outside treads wear while the inner treads remain normal. Check tire pressure before someone talks you into an expensive job when the problem could be no more than your tires being over- or underinflated. Worn steering-linkage parts like the idler arm, tie rod, center link, bushings—these allow the tire to oscillate from side to side, causing gouges in the tire tread. Unbalanced wheels, which could compound the problem of a worn linkage, actually look like someone has taken a scalloper and cut gouges right out of your tire in a perfectly formed set of little scallops on the sides. If you see this, look for more than just an alignment. You are going to need some changes in parts.

Breaking In Your Tires   Most people are not aware that tires, like a pair of shoes, have to be broken in. I have heard people say, "I am going to put new tires on the car because I am going on a long trip." And the day before the trip, they put on four new tires and immediately drive at 50, 60, or 70 mph. This is the most prevalent cause of tire breakage and of separation of the rubber from the cord inner part of the tire. A car with new tires should be run for 50 or 60 miles at normal temperatures and at normal speeds—25 to 35 mph. You should never go over 60 mph for the first 50 miles. If you do, you will shorten the life of the tires. You will cause the kind of separation that leaves your tread all over the road while you cuss out the tire company. This is particularly true of steel-belted tires. Steel belts can act like tiny razor blades inside the tire when there is a stretching or tension. The steel cuts the rubber, and the rubber tread separates from the steel belt of the tire. Allowing the tire to break in with normal city driving for 50 or 60 miles at 25 or 30 mph before putting it on the road at high speeds increases the life of your tires. Race-car drivers have known this for years, but average motorists have not been aware of it because they have never been told. Now you have been told.

I am constantly asked how you get the body-shop owner to pick up the $100, $200, or $250 that the insurance company wants you to pay if you have an accident. My answer is, *don't do it*! When you ask the body-shop owner "to bury the deductible," you are asking for a second-rate job. Body-shop operators face this request all the time, and at this point they really should advise the car owner, "Yes, I can bury the $100, $200, or $250, but I'm going to use used parts, or give one coat of paint instead of three, or I'm going to cut corners somewhere else."

Let's face it, the insurance people who set the limits on how much is going to be paid for your accident know what it will cost to fix your car. They are experts. Now, when you ask to bury $200 or $250 in a $650, $800, or even a $1,000 job, the body-shop person has to do it in some way that is going to satisfy the insurance company and you that the work was done and still come out with some kind of profit. Obviously, cutting the price on the job by 25% is not going to leave much of a profit, so what can be done? Well, you have to realize that a person willing to cheat an insurance company is probably equally willing to cheat you, the car owner. Because a body shop never simply absorbs that deductible; the value is taken right out of the job, and the car owner takes the loss in several ways. If the job is not done properly, the car is worth less when you want to sell it. If it is not painted properly, the paint may crack, split, peel, or chip six months down the road. If first-rate repairs were not made, you might be stuck with old used parts, which although not always all bad, nevertheless remind you of their existence.

Another very important item. Conspiring to bury the deductible is committing fraud on the insurance company. You are breaking the law, and so is the body-shop owner. Insurance company appraisers are the best around, and they know the cost of repairs. You are not going to beat them, you are only going to beat yourself.

And one last quick point: If the body-shop owner does decide to bury the deductible, he will buy used parts, and in today's market that means that a thief just got rich by stealing somebody's car to obtain parts for yours.

Let's look at a phenomenon that is beginning to happen around the country—the diagnostic center operated by a disinterested party. AAA has opened several diagnostic clinics, and it is a good idea. Put out $35, and they go over your car stem to stern, top to bottom, and will tell you everything that is wrong with your car—and everything that is right, too. There is one problem, they can be very picky, particularly if you own an older car. People who drive older cars and just want to make sure the safety factors like brakes and tires are all right, who want to make sure the car runs so they can keep it another year or two, are not interested in some complex diagnostic problems. I have seen people actually afraid to get back into their cars after AAA had finished with them, even though their cars were serviceable.

What to fix depends on what you need the car for. If all you do is go to the store and back, everything on the safety end is okay, and the car is running, you're fine. Problems with safety equipment, however, are a different story and definitely should be fixed. But when AAA says you are burning oil or have bad valves or a few other things that can scare the daylights out of somebody with an older car, you may or may not want to worry about it.

Should you use one of these centers? You should consider taking your car to a diagnostic center such as AAA's if you are not sure you have a top mechanic or are afraid that your mechanic will rip you off. This way you can obtain a list of exactly what is wrong with the car and get the mechanic's prices for doing exactly those jobs. The diagnostic center does go deeply into the car, and the mechanic will not be able to come back to you and say he found something else wrong. If anything is wrong, the diagnostic center will find it and tell you about it.

THE DO-IT-YOURSELF MANUAL FOR PEOPLE WHO NEVER DO ANYTHING THEMSELVES

Chapter 8

YOUR CAR IN ALL SEASONS

To keep your car running all year it must be serviced properly for each weather change. For instance, when summer is on the way, it is time to begin thinking of preparing your car for hot weather. The most important preparation is to check the cooling system. Your coolant level and cooling system should be up to par all the time but especially when you are getting ready for summer.

First of all, take the cap off the radiator *only* when you are able to place your palm flat down on the cap without feeling intense heat. If you try to take the cap off while the radiator is hot, you will wind up spraying yourself and everything in sight with hot radiator coolant. And that's no fun.

When you have the cap off, take a good look at the radiator coolant. How is its color? It should be a shade of green. A yellow tinge may be present, but you should not see rust. If you see a rust color, the radiator needs a flush. You can do it yourself with items for sale at a good auto-parts store, or you can have a mechanic do it for you. Either way, if the coolant has been in the car 2 years or more, or if you see rust, you should have the radiator flushed.

When you add new coolant, do not let somebody sell you an entire cooling system full of antifreeze or coolant. A 50-50 mix is what you want—half water and half antifreeze. That mix is what you need in most of the United States, and it actually cools better in hot weather and protects better in winter. Whether it is winter or summer, a 50-50 mix is the best way to go. You will save a lot of money if you buy the antifreeze and anything else you need at a good auto-parts store.

Certain other parts of your car are affected by heat and should be checked out. For instance, how are your ignition wires? Have they been on for a couple of years now? Today's cars run very hot, and summer and wet weather can be hard on old wires. For a reasonable enough price at any auto-parts store, you can buy a set of wires for the summer that will last another 2 years. Summer is the best time to look for this kind of item.

Tires Another seasonal task, and one I really should have started with, is the removal of snow tires. If you are using all-weather tires, there is no need to take them off. They are made for year-round use, but if you have snow tires on, get them off. (When you have decided to replace any tires on your car, realize that if you have radials on the front, you need radials on the back. If you have bias-ply tires on the front, you need bias-ply tires on the back. Regardless of what kind you have, all four must be the same.)

Time for a Tune-up? The arrival of warm weather is a good time to have your car tuned up. It has had a rough winter and probably picked up water in the gas tank as a result of condensation because of the cold weather. This is the time to add that final can of gasoline antifreeze to your tank and also check the plugs—little jobs you can do for yourself.

Pull the plugs. See what they look like. Do they look clean? Do they look as if everything is burning fine? Or do you see corrosion, oil, or other contaminants on the plugs? Do they look burned out? If they do, buy a set of good spark plugs and put them in, a simple operation in today's cars. Many, many times you will also want to replace other items on the car, and your owner's manual can tell you what to do. In many cases, you can do the job yourself and save that $30 or $40 tune-up. Remember: The biggest and easiest part of a tune-up is changing the plugs.

This does not mean you should skimp on regular tune-ups. Your car should be put on the electronic analyzer at least once a year in order to bring everything up to factory specifications. At the same time, the air-pollution equipment should be checked and cleaned along with all vacuum lines.

Safety Check Are you due to have your car safety checked? In states with mandatory inspections, people complain about being ripped off at inspection stations. An easy way to avoid this is to examine the car before you go in. Does your horn work? It's a bad idea to wait until the inspection person tells you it does not. Do windshield washers and wipers spray correctly and wipe clean? Check exterior lights by having someone stand outside the car to see whether the turn signals, brake lights, back-up lights, and all other lights are working properly. Nobody can tell you that he or she had to replace bulbs in your car if all lights were working when you checked just before you went in for your inspection. Little unnecessary repairs are an easy way for some service stations to rip you off for a couple of bucks.

Conquer Overheating!

Summertime, even with a well-prepared car, can be rough. For instance, if you run the air conditioner in traffic, which you might do every day, you run the risk of overheating. Do you know what to do when your car overheats? Do you know how to get the problem fixed and how to get the car moving when it happens?

Let's start with what happens and what you should do. Here you are in stop-and-start traffic, and suddenly the red dashboard light goes on. The car begins to chug a little, and you smell a little burning of that glycol antifreeze. What do you do?

1. Turn off the air conditioner.
2. Shift the car into neutral and put your foot on the gas. That's right, on the gas. Get the engine running faster. Get the fan spinning faster.
3. This step is the one that is going to hurt — put your heater on.

I *know* it is hot, I *know* you have to open all the windows, that you are going to perspire through your new shirt . . . but put the heater on before the car dies totally in traffic. By turning on the heat, you bring the heat from the engine into the car and dissipate it. Once you have taken these steps, you will see the red light go out very quickly, or the temperature gauge, if you have one, drop very quickly. And when you get back into moving traffic, you can probably go back to using your air conditioner. Sitting around waiting in traffic caused the overheating.

When you get the car home, after you have the radiator flushed and add new coolant, you will most likely have to put in a new thermostat.

Do put a thermostat in the car. Any good repair manual for your car will tell you how to put it in. It is there for a good reason. People who tell you to take it out in the summer are wrong. It is important that the thermostat hold the water in the radiator to cool the engine in hot weather. Just as important, the thermostat must hold the water in the engine block in winter to warm the engine. So, get a proper thermostat and put it in—in the summer.

Finally, and most importantly, check the fan. If the fan clutches are gone or if the fan is not spinning properly, it can cause a lot of overheating, too. An easy way to check it is to grab one blade and spin it. If the fan spins more than four or five times without stopping, you know your clutches are gone and need to be replaced.

Get Ready for Winter

Winter is a wonderful time of year. Kids playing outside with the sleighs, everyone goes over the fields to Grandma's house, sleigh bells ring—and you look out the window and wonder, "How am I going to get to work?" In winter children frolic, and you think constantly of the problems you are sure to have with your car.

This year could be different. You can decide to prevent many of those problems before they happen. I will deal with winter car troubles and what you should do ahead of time to avoid getting stuck later on. Getting yourself and your car ready for cold weather is not as easy as you think. But the trouble you take is worthwhile because people who go into winter passively waiting for something to happen to their cars, invariably get what they are asking for—trouble.

Added Weight Some people put extra weight in the rear end of their cars to get more traction. Not a bad idea, but certain factors should be taken into account. The extra weight—cinder blocks, bags of sand, a small elephant—can help improve low-speed traction on a rear-wheel-drive car. (Never put weight in the rear of a front-wheel-drive car. It already has plenty of weight up front over the driving wheels with the engine.) Too much weight, however, can adversely affect the car's handling. Overloading upsets the balance of the vehicle, making it prone to skidding during cornering on slippery surfaces, and possibly even on not-so-slippery surfaces. If you put weight in the back of a rear-wheel-drive car, you should not use more than 100 lbs. for the average car, and if you have a smaller vehicle, less weight is desirable. The overall weight of a vehicle must be taken into consideration—75 lbs. for subcompacts; 100 lbs. for compacts or intermediates; up to, but never over, 150 lbs. for large cars. (Throughout this section, I will suggest some useful supplies to keep in the trunk of your car that will add weight in a natural form, which makes more sense than loading up with cinder blocks or sand.)

Supplies for Snow and Ice Before cold weather settles in to stay, you should equip you car with several *must* supplies. Some are ordinary, some you may not have thought of. They will give you that extra weight and also prove useful. A set of **strap-on chains** in the trunk of your car is always a good item. Even if it never snows, they will not go bad and will be there should you ever need them. A **shovel,** one of those inexpensive folding trench shovels you can get in an army surplus store, is also useful as are a **snow brush, ice scraper,** and **sand,** something that will help you add weight while serving a useful function. Carry the sand in used plastic gallon milk bottles. Bottles of sand do not get all over the floor of your trunk and are easier to remove than a large, heavy bag. One gallon-bottle of sand should get you out of any spot if you get stuck.

Here is a point about which I disagree with a great many so-called experts. Never carry salt in the trunk compartment of your car. Reasons?

1. Moisture in the trunk that causes the salt to work on the metal or rug of the trunk could wind up giving the car holes down through the gas tank. This has happened.
2. Salt is more expensive than sand, yet on a cold, icy day

when you need traction to get out of a tight spot, sand is just as effective.

3. Salt works only after it melts, which takes time. When you put salt under your wheels, you may as well take a little nap while it melts the snow or ice under those wheels.

Battery Check-up In the winter the battery takes its toughest beating. Cold weather causes batteries to lose power. In the arctic north, drivers keep a battery charger on the car at all times when it is parked because the temperature frequently sinks below zero. In cold weather, batteries do not put out as much and cannot hold as heavy a charge to start the car. It is imperative to keep a check on your battery and make sure it is strong. Going into the winter with a weak battery is looking for trouble.

Protecting the Engine You should avoid heavy-weight oils during winter. Low temperatures cause them to thicken up, causing an added strain on an already weakened battery during cold starts. New cars use a multiple or variable-viscosity oil such as 10W40, which adapts to temperature changes without a problem. Heavy-weight oil, especially single-weight oil like 30, 40, or 50, can be used in older high-mileage cars in warm weather. In winter, however, it should be replaced with a light-weight variable-viscosity oil like 10W40. If you have a car that uses too much oil, you can go to a 20W50, which might also be good if your car has a lot of miles on it. In winter, you are far better off with a variable-viscosity oil and nothing heavier at the low end than a 20W.

Frigid temperatures cause moisture to collect in the fuel system, which can freeze up and block the flow of gas through the lines. Freezing is a very important factor with diesel fuel as well as with gasoline. Several brands of gas antifreeze on the market prevent the problem by removing the moisture from the fuel. They are made up of an alcohol compound. (Alcohol and water mix and can be burned by the engine just as though the mixture were alcohol alone.) Under normal winter conditions with temperatures between 0° and 30°F, you should add about one can of a gas-drying mixture to every three or four tankfuls of gas. If you get down below half a tank, you really ought to fill it. Diesel owners can buy special diesel fuel conditioners, but check the owner's manual before using them.

Myths abound about what to do with tires in cold, icy, snowy weather. For example, tire pressure is one of the most critical, most misunderstood, and most often neglected factors influencing the performance of an automobile. It affects wear, ride, traction, braking, cornering ability, and winter driving. A constant check with an accurate gauge is absolutely required to keep the tires at the pressure recommended by the manufacturer. During winter, a closer than usual watch is necessary. If you had your tires checked a couple of weeks ago when the temperature was in the 80s and today when the temperature was in the 50s, you would have discovered that your tires lost three pounds of air pressure. For every 10 degrees the temperature drops, you lose a pound of air pressure. Given day-to-day variations in temperature, particularly in fall and winter, it pays to keep a constant check on the tires to make sure they are properly inflated.

Of Tires and Chains Many people have the dangerous idea they can let air out of the tires to obtain more traction on ice and snow. This is not so. If you happen to be plowing through deep snow, letting some air out can do some good, but once you get out of the deep snow, having low air pressure can actually cause you to skid more than you would with the proper air pressure. If you do let the air out of the tires to get out of deep snow, put the air back in the tires before you return to the highway or any surface that is slick. You will not be able to control a car with low tire pressure if you are on an icy, snowy highway.

Front-wheel-drive cars perform far better in snow than rear-wheel-drive cars because the engine weight is over those driving wheels. **Radials** might prove sufficient on a front-wheel-drive car but if you opt for **snow tires** put them on all four wheels to maintain the same degree of traction all around and discourage the rear from sliding out. In most parts of the country, it is not necessary to go to that extreme. Good **all-weather tires** are sufficient—at all four corners. This will give plenty of traction and keep the rear from swinging around to meet the front. Be careful when driving and have good all-season tires on the front-wheel-drive car, and you should not have a problem. (Later, I will discuss how to handle your car in snow and ice for both front- and rear-wheel-drive cars.)

Chains are difficult to put on in the very weather in which they are supposed to work. They are noisy and cannot be used on open highways, where they burn right off. **Studded tires** provide three times the traction of nonstudded tires on ice but are not as effective as chains. In some states, studded tires are still banned, and 25 states limit the months in which studded tires can be used. When you do any traveling, study the laws carefully if you use studded tires on your car. There are special **compound tires** that stay pliable at low temperatures and prove to be quite effective on ice but fall below chains and studs in effectiveness.

What should you use? For most areas of the country, the snow tire is the most effective winter accident deterrent. Most areas do not get enough snow to warrant your spending money on a full set of chains and then figuring out how to put them on in a blizzard. There are alternatives to chains. For example, the so-called **strap-chains** are a type of chain consisting of only one or two straps of chain that you put on the tire when it snows. They go on fairly easily and come off smoothly. In the morning, when you come out and the snow is heavy on the ground, you can put the chains on quickly and then stop for a moment to take them off when you reach the open highway. By the time you start home at night, enough traffic will have gone through your street so that you will not have to put them on again. Strap chains can be put on over snow tires, are easy to use, and can be found at most good auto-parts stores. Strap chains generally provide plenty of protection in most parts of the country.

Handling a Winter Breakdown

What do you do if your vehicle does become disabled out on the road in the cold of winter? Unless you are sure of where you are and where help can be found, stay with the car. Do not venture out for help in below-freezing temperatures unless you know that you can reach help easily on foot. Even a cold car provides protection from the elements. The wind will not whip you, the snow will not get your feet and clothes wet. For cold-weather emergencies, always keep flares and a piece of cloth in your trunk or glove compartment. When you get stuck, place one flare on the road far enough behind your car to warn oncoming motorists of your location. Then, lift the hood and tie a cloth, preferably a light-colored one, on the antenna or door handle of your car—this signals your plight. Flares and a piece of cloth are useful year-round, and they are absolutely essential when the weather is cold because the sooner someone who can help spots you, the better off you will be.

Tip: If the motor is still running and you have the heater on, be sure you open at least one window an inch or so, no matter how cold it is outside. Having the heater on in a stalled car can cause you to suffocate.

You can bet that as you go along the road, if the cars in front are spewing muck onto your windshield, they are doing the same to your headlights. And your own car is probably throwing a lot of muck over your own taillights. For night driving, you better clean off the car's headlights and taillights. This is essential so that you can see where you are going, and other drivers can see you coming toward them. If you are on a salted, sanded, snowy, icy highway, those lights will get badly covered without your realizing it.

Be certain to keep the windshield, side windows, back window, headlights, and taillights clear. Too often in winter weather, you see a guy with tunnel vision—because he has restricted his vision to a little clear patch on the driver's side of his windshield. He wipes off just enough snow and muck in the front to see straight ahead and does not clear off the back or side windows at all. Be smart. Keep a snow brush in the car—and use it—or you are heading for an accident.

Your Breakdown Wardrobe Here are some other items to keep in the trunk of the car to keep you going in the wintertime. Sitting in the car when it has stalled along the side of the road can get awfully cold. If you have a breakdown in the winter, you want something to help you stay warm. A change of clothes, *very warm clothes,* should be carried at all times during the winter. You know when you will have a flat—not until you are driving home from the New Year's Eve ball all dressed up in your tuxedo or evening coat. So, it is not a bad idea to have a pair of heavy pants, an old heavy coat, and some warm gloves to change that inevitable flat. If your car gets stuck, and the engine quits, you can use those clothes to keep you warm inside the car. Your special breakdown wardrobe should also include a warm hat, ear protection, and thermal underwear. If you can't imagine changing clothes in the car, think again. When you get a little cold, you will be happy to change if you have some thermal underwear handy. Heavy socks, boots, a coat, a sweater, pants, gloves, and even a sleeping bag are good protection to have along if you expect to do any traveling. If you drive outside populated areas in winter, a sleeping bag in the trunk could save your life, should you get stuck in a snowstorm in the middle of nowhere with your car. If you are marooned in your car and cannot keep warm, you could get tired, fall asleep, and risk freezing to death. It cannot be put any simpler than that.

Getting Going

How long should your engine warm up and should you use overnight engine warmers in winter? You can get as many different opinions on how long it takes to warm up a car in cold weather as there are people on your block. Actually, there is no set pattern for warming up your car. With gas as expensive as it is, allowing a car to sit outside and run at idle for 5, 10, or 15 minutes is blowing your money out the exhaust pipe. The best procedure is to start the car, let it sit for no more than a minute, and then proceed at a slow pace. In cold weather, do not try to dig out and really move while the car is still cold. The car will stall, buck, and fight you. Also, it is not good to let an engine run for a long period at a fast idle after a cold start. The inner workings of the motor will not be properly lubricated because the oil is still thick from a cold night of inactivity, when it was lying at the bottom of the engine. An idle does not bring that oil up. You must be moving to get the oil through the engine properly. Pouring large amounts of gas into the engine, which is what the high idle does, can actually wash down the sides of the cylinders and wash away the oil that ought to be there. You also have a good chance of fouling the spark plugs. So, idle the car for about a minute, move off in a normal manner, and do not press the car too hard.

A sure way to get an instant start on cold mornings is to put in an engine heater. Engine heaters are convenient devices and available in many varieties:

1. The bolt type that replaces a standard bolt in the engine block
2. A cooling-system heater, which is a small heating device placed into the hose between the radiator and engine block
3. The oil heater, a device that replaces the oil dip stick when it is in use.

In most areas of the country, the weather does not get cold enough to require one of these heaters. If you think you could use one, though, they are not too expensive.

The Infamous Frozen Door Lock   How many people call into work to say, "I cannot get into my car. The locks are frozen"? You can avoid this by thinking ahead and spraying a graphite powder into the lock when it is dry and working well. Any locksmith and most auto-parts stores carry graphite powder. You can also place an adhesive bandage over the lock to keep out moisture when it is snowing or raining. It works. Unfreezing a lock can be accomplished with the old heat-the-key-with-a-match trick, or by using a modern version of the match—an inexpensive lighter. As a last resort, you can cup your hands around the lock and breathe on it.

Never use oil in the lock during the winter. Oil gets sticky and thick when the temperature drops, and nothing will help a lock stuck up with cold oil except applying heat.

Safe Winter Driving

How do you learn to control your car in all types of driving conditions?

Everything begins with feel. You must learn your car's idio-syncrasies. You must learn to read the messages it sends to you through the steering wheel, learn the feel of the seats and the feel of the whole car and its movement while you drive. If you do not get the feel of your car, you will never be able to deal with dangerous situations. When you get into a car for the first time, be extra careful. Every car has different tendencies, particularly from make to make and model to model. Even when a friend drives exactly the same make and model as you, he or she may have a different tire tread or a worn set of tires. The car will not handle the same as yours. Handling and feel are something you have to learn for yourself.

Sitting Correctly   You will not be able to feel and react to any of the messages the car sends you if you slouch in the seat with two fingers on the wheel and your mind in the clouds. When you drive in any kind of weather, particularly bad, have a grip on that steering wheel and sit up straight. Sit in a comfortable position, not in a stiff military posture or one that gives you a backache. You should be comfortable, yet you cannot control a car if your back is not firmly against the seat, your feet firmly on the pedals, and your hands firmly gripping the wheel.

Driving Techniques   A driver who grips a wheel so tightly that his or her knuckles become white does not have control. Hands can freeze at that position because the muscles are too tense. Most steering wheels have spokes between the 10 o'clock and 2 o'clock or 9 o'clock and 3 o'clock positions, and driving instructors usually recommend that you hook your thumbs lightly over these nearly horizontal spokes. All racing drivers hold the wheel that way because it gives them an excellent feel for what the front tires are doing plus a little extra leverage to turn the wheel—more leverage than just grabbing the rim of the wheel provides. It also prevents losing your grip if the steering column is wrenched away when the car hits a violent bump or an irregularity in the road.

Important, too, is the input of the pedals, especially the brakes. Push or squeeze the brake with the ball of your foot. Do not get the brake pedal hooked between the heel and ball of your foot. Do not use the arch, which has less feeling than the ball. When you depress the brakes with the ball of your foot, you can feel what is happening to the brakes more quickly. You know immediately when they lock up on you. If you have a manual-shift car, the shift lever should be gently guided, push in with the palm, pull it with the fingers into each gear.

Do not grip it like a baseball bat and jam it back and forth. Control motions should be smooth. When you have a rough input, whether it be in the steering, throttle, brake, or clutch, it causes a sudden weight transfer of the car and can cause you to skid. A front-wheel-drive car is normally balanced with 60% of its weight on the front wheels and 40% on the rear wheels, and rear-wheel-drive vehicles have a front-to-rear weight ratio of 55:45. Suddenly hitting the brake or throttle can shift that weight percentage by 20% to 30%. This means you could be throwing 90% of the car's weight onto the front wheels of a front-wheel-drive car by attempting a sudden stop.

Skidding How do you drive safely in winter on snow and ice? Beginning with skidding, let's look at some of the typical situations you could encounter and how to get out of them. Practice makes perfect, yet it is difficult to practice skids. Knowing what happens when you go into skids, however, helps you to prevent them and, when they occur, to regain control of your car.

There are two types of skids, the "understeer," or front-wheel, skid, and the "oversteer," or rear-wheel, skid, and they are two situations you can run into in everyday driving. "Understeer" means the car wants to keep going in the direction it is headed. If you are coming off an expressway or trying to turn on a curved highway, you discover that you are fighting the car, which wants to keep going straight. The front wheels are fighting you by starting to skid while the rear continues to push forward. "Oversteer" is the opposite. It happens when you turn your wheels hard in one direction and discover that your rear wheels have let go and are facing in the direction you are turning more quickly than you anticipated. On a very slippery surface, you may even go into a complete spin.

The Understeer Skid As front-wheel-drive cars have become popular, understeer skids have become the bigger problem. The front-wheel-drive car is heavily weighted to the front end. As I mentioned above, approximately 60% of all the weight is on the front of the car and over the driving wheels. In snow, these cars generally react well

127

because the weight distribution adds to traction. The trouble is, however, that they do tend to understeer.

Having all that weight up front gives you excellent traction and makes the car go in a beautifully straight line. Like a dart with a weighted tip, the car wants to go straight. Which means that it does not turn very well. Today's power steering and other mechanical advances obscure the fact that your car is difficult to turn until you find yourself faced with a skid. You are on a curving road, going at a fairly good speed, and you try to make a hard turn, only to realize that the car wants to continue going in a straight line. Or you hit a patch of ice and suddenly discover there is no way you are going to make the car turn. In both scenarios, you enter an understeer skid. With the rear end so light, when you hit one of these skids, it comes around and tries to meet you in front because there is nothing holding it down.

Front-wheel-drive cars can give excellent traction in winter weather, but you must learn to drive and control them. The most important things to know are exactly what your car can do and will not do. A front-wheel-drive car that loses traction in the front on ice is not going to turn. It is not going to do anything but skid until you can slow it down and make those tires bite. Remember, the tires in front turn and drive the car. When they lose traction, you lose both turning ability and braking ability. You must also realize that when you hit the brakes too hard, you lock up those front wheels and again lose both turning and braking ability.

Assume you are going into an understeer skid. What do you do? The key to controlling a front-wheel skid is to transfer the weight of the car forward. Make the weight of the car push down on the front wheels, helping them regain traction. How? By easing off the throttle and, if necessary, squeezing *gently* on the brake. Fortunately, when you start to skid you usually do take your foot off the throttle. It's the second part of your response that takes thought and concentration. You want to hit the brakes but not in panic. Remember, *squeeze* them. Do not tromp on them. Restraint is what we are talking about. If you hit the brakes too hard or too suddenly, you will lock up the front wheels and lose all steering control. If this happens, ease off the brakes until the tires stop skidding and start steering. Gently squeeze the brakes again if necessary, keeping the braking force just below the point of lockup. Gentle pumping of the brakes combined with steering in the right direction should take care of any normal understeer condition.

Above all, you must react carefully—pump your brakes. Learn to *feel* how hard they should be pumped. If each time you pump the brakes the wheels lock up and the tires break loose again, then you are in more trouble than when you started. In a front-wheel-drive car you have one other advantage—you can use a little throttle to get the front tires pulling you through the turn. If you give too much gas, however, you will lose traction and start spinning. So, ease off a bit until you feel the tires rolling and gripping the road as they should.

The Oversteer Skid   This type of skid is trickier to control because of your natural reaction—getting off the gas and stepping on the brakes, transferring the car's weight forward, away from the skidding tires—makes the situation worse.

The first crucial thing to remember is never to touch the brakes in an oversteer condition. When your rear end starts coming at you, do not hit the brakes. If the skid was caused by too much braking in the first place, get off the brakes immediately and stay off until the skid is under control.

Steering is the second critical factor. You have heard that you should turn into the skid. This means turning the front wheels in the same direction that the rear end is sliding. Try to get both ends of the car going the same way or you will wind up in a spin.

This must be done immediately and decisively.

Turn the wheel fast to stop the rear from pivoting around to the front. If you can do these two things—stay off the brakes and steer hard and fast the way the rear is skidding—you can catch almost any potential spin.

Once you have caught the skid, however, the job is not quite done. Even experienced race drivers lose control because they do not anticipate the second, often more violent, skid that usually follows in the opposite direction from the initial skid. You have seen people fishtailing down the road going one way and then the other. They are not able to control the second skid. When you have caught the rear and it starts back to where it should be, immediately crank the steering wheel just as quickly and decisively back the other way to counteract this second skid. That is how you return the steering to front and center.

No driving technique by itself is more important than knowing your car. Although it is difficult to practice skidding, you can learn how your car "feels" in all types of weather. Especially in those front-heavy, front-drive cars, you must be very careful not to take your foot off the gas pedal too quickly when you go into an oversteer condition. Lifting your foot is just like braking: it transfers the weight of the car. The traction then leaves the rear tires, which can make a rear-wheel slide worse. This situation is known as "trailing throttle oversteer." It is not important to remember the term. However, be familiar with the condition. It is common to all cars but much worse in front-drive cars or in rear-engine, rear-drive cars like the Porsche or the old VW. Most of us experience mild oversteer in rear-drive cars, when we start those rear tires spinning with too much gas. Easing off on the gas to regain traction while steering into the skid solves that problem. But beware of trailing throttle oversteer if your drive wheels are in front. When the rear wheels start to slide, it is best to leave the throttle where it is and concentrate on the steering. If you remain cool enough, you will find that adding a little throttle—that is, hitting the gas a little in an oversteering front-drive car—helps pull the rear back in line. In rear-drive cars you do get off the throttle a little when you go into a skid. But in a front-drive car taking your foot off the gas pedal will increase the action of the skid. You should stay on the gas and keep those wheels moving because they will help pull you out of the skid.

Wet Weather Driving Tips

Obviously, good tires are a must. Obviously, good brakes are a must, too. Yet a film of water on the road negates the advantages of both those things and makes driving a totally different ball of wax. Realize that weather conditions are all-important to your driving habits. Learn to drive differently when road conditions change.

When driving in wet weather, it is important to realize that it does not take a lot of rain to make the roads slippery. In fact, sometimes the most slippery time in a rainstorm is when it first starts, because grime and grease accumulate on the road. In particular, places where a lot of cars have stopped, especially at stop signs and red lights, become just like soap or ice when you hit them after the start of rain. Later on in a rainstorm, much of the slippery stuff has been washed away, and the road is not as bad. In the early part of a storm, be exceedingly careful when pulling up to a stop, and always slow down when it rains because the stopping distances on wet streets are 25% to 30% longer than on dry streets.

Another big problem in rainy weather is hydroplaning. When you go at a high speed on a wet road, your front tires may actually ride on a thin layer of water, just as if you were on water skis. You have no control over your car when that happens. You risk drifting to one side and going into a spin, at which point a number of bad things can happen. If you ever feel your front wheels start to drift, take your foot off the gas. Do not touch the brakes or turn the wheel. As you slow down, the wheels will get back to the road surface, and you will be in control of the car again.

Most importantly, avoid those sudden moves. Probably the most dangerous things you can do in wet weather are turn the wheel or hit the brakes suddenly. Be especially careful on turns. Your car does not react on wet roads the same way it does on dry roads. Going into a turn in wet weather the same way you do in dry weather could result in losing the rear end of the car and doing a complete 360° spin.

Fog   If you cannot avoid being on the road in fog, put on your low-beam headlights instead of the high beams, which reflect right back at you from the fog, allowing you to see less road and more glare. The low beams show you more road and less glare.

If you are the nervous type, buy yourself a set of fog lights for the front of your car. They should go below the headlights, but no less than 12 inches off the ground, and they should be aimed properly. Too often, when fog lights are put on a car, even when a mechanic does the job, they wind up pointing up, down, or to the side, and not toward the road. Use your defroster because you are going to get condensation on the inside of your windshield on almost any foggy day. Be especially alert for oncoming cars through that rearview mirror. If you stop abruptly, the car behind you might land into you. Keep moving. Certainly you must slow down, but do not slow down to the point where cars coming up behind you are going to kiss your tail.

Chapter 9

EASY REPAIRS FOR EVERYONE

10 Self-service Checks You Can Perform without Tools

You say you are all thumbs, you can't fix anything, and you can't even boil water? Well, most of the repairs your car needs are as simple as wrapping a package, or taking the temperature of a child. So many skills that you use every day can easily be transferred to working on your car. Not only are typical car problems fairly simple to solve, the tools and other supplies you need are also easy to obtain and use. And you can begin to equip yourself for basic preventive tests and general repairs for about $20 to $25, even with today's inflation.

Many people try to save a couple of extra pennies on every gallon of gasoline at self-service gas stations. The problem is that self-service means No Service under the hood. Nobody checks your tire pressure, oil, and water, nobody wipes your windshield, nobody does nothin' anymore. And strangely enough, when you stop at an island that says "full service," the same thing is liable to happen—they still won't check your oil, water, tires, or answer your questions. Which means that you ought to get into the habit of routinely checking these items yourself. You will need a good tire gauge, a pair of light work-gloves, and some old rags, tissues, or paper towels (and possibly a screwdriver, if your fan belt turns out to be loose and you decide to go ahead and tighten it).

Your car sends you messages if you listen for them. Your car constantly gives you information about its condition. The question is, Do you understand what it is saying? And what can you do about it? These 10 self-service checks, if you make them part of your daily relationship with your car, will teach you how to listen to and understand your car's "language."

Checking the Brakes You should wonder at all times whether your brakes are safe. Even a reliable service-station attendant cannot do this wondering for you. Are you one of those people who never bother to check? It is something you can do for yourself.

Push the pedal down. If it goes more than halfway to the floor without meeting resistance, that is too far. The brake pedal should feel like it is hitting something hard. If its feel is soft and mushy, you have a problem, usually air in the brake lines.

Now, the second check. Push the brake pedal down hard and hold your foot down. If the pedal hits something and keeps slowly going down, you could have trouble.

For power brakes, of course, you have to have the engine running to do these tests. With mechanical brakes you can do them with the engine off. If there is anything suspicious at all, fix it yourself if you are a good mechanic, or take the car to an expert to have it fixed.

Checking for Leaks Now, what about those little drips and drops, the ones that you spot on your driveway or out in front of the house where you park your car? Are they a problem? They could be. The easiest way to find out is to spread some paper under your car at night, holding it down with some rocks. The next day, you will be able to see from the locations of any spots on the paper exactly where the leaks are.

Clear, condensed water from the air conditioner is no problem and perfectly normal. If anything else is dripping, however, it could mean something is wrong. For instance, red or light brownish fluid leaking from your transmission should be checked. Black, oily fluid—obviously oil—also should be checked. You might be able to locate its source yourself very simply by cleaning down the engine with one of the new engine-cleaning sprays, driving the car for a few miles, and then seeing where you have streaks of oil. That could tell you where that leak is coming from.

Checking the Oil First, find out where the dip stick is for your car, pull it out, and check the oil. Very simply, take out the dip stick, wipe it on a piece of rag or paper towel until it is clean, and put it back into the car. Then, pull it out once more and see where the oil level is. If it falls between "add" and "full," you have enough oil. If you can read the word "add," put in a quart of oil. This is easy enough to do, and if you are at a service station when you check your oil, they will add the oil for you because they make a few cents on the quart you buy.

Checking the Radiator   If the car is hot, don't open the radiator cap—that's important. Most new cars have a plastic overflow tank that you can see through without touching anything. Find the "full cold" and "full hot" marks. If the water or coolant reads anywhere between those marks, everything is fine. If the cannister is low or empty, fill it to the "full cold" mark and check it again in a day or so.

Checking Power-Steering Fluid   Locate the power-steering pump. Because it is difficult to find, many people forget about it. This pump, with its reservoir, is usually on the driver's side and connected by a drive belt to the engine. Once you find it, wipe the dirt off the cap and remove it. Generally speaking, there is a little dip stick built right into the top of the reservoir cap. If not, you can tell where the fluid is by markings along the side of the reservoir neck. One way or the other, it's not hard to tell the fluid level, and usually filling it is only a matter of a couple of ounces of power-steering fluid, which is the same stuff as automatic-transmission fluid. If you prefer, however, special power-steering fluids are available at your auto-parts store that are probably a little better than using plain ATF. Also, they are a little less messy because they come in easy-pour cans.

Checking Transmission Fluid   Generally, for this test the car must be in neutral or park, the engine must be idling and must have been warmed up for a while. Usually, you will find the dip stick for your automatic transmission at the rear of the engine on the passenger side. Pull the dip stick, wipe it off, put it back in, and read as you would when checking the oil. If the fluid is above the "add" line, it is fine. If you can read the word "add," you probably need about a pint of fluid. Try a pint first, and if you still need some, add it in much smaller increments. Overfilling a transmission can damage it. In most cases, other fluid reservoirs are not hurt too much by overfilling, but a transmission is very temperamental. This one you must be careful with.

Checking the Tires   The next thing—check your tires. This is a very important test, which is why I suggest you have a tire gauge. Keep those tires inflated, and you will be sure to have more mileage and longer wear from them.

Caution: Today's front-wheel-drive cars with the engines set sideways have the dip sticks and other items to be checked in different places from those in the old-style cars. Check your owner's manual for the proper locations.

Checking the Dashboard Lights   When you turn the key in your car, do your dashboard warning lights work? This is a good time to check. They should all light up when you turn the key and first crank the car just before it actually starts up. This is a common check, yet not all drivers bother to learn what dashboard lights are and what they indicate. Check the owner's manual of your car, because those lights are all-important—they can tell you the condition of your car at a glance.

Checking the Fan Belt   You can save yourself a lot of heartache and sometimes a lot of money in a rip-off on parts like voltage regulators, alternators, and batteries simply by checking your fan belt. Many, many times there is nothing wrong with an automobile other than a loose fan belt, which in turn causes a starting problem, a low battery, or another seemingly serious problem. The rule of thumb here is to use your thumb. Just take your thumb and press it down on the fan belt. You should not be able to push down more than a half inch without meeting real resistance. If the fan belt does resist after just a half inch, it is good and tight. If you go down more than that, the fan belt needs to be tightened. Do it yourself, or take the car somewhere to have the job done.

Checking the Battery and Battery Cables   Many people pay good money for new batteries and other electronic components when all they need is a good set of cables. Check to see whether the battery cables are frayed or have white gook on them. When you have good, clean cables, your battery can give you its best.

Checking the battery is a two-step process.

1. Check the fluid level. Do not smoke when you do this as batteries give off an explosive gas. Take the cap off, make sure the solution inside comes up to the bottom of the filler neck. When it is at the right level, the fluid touches the filler neck then puckers a little bit. It looks as though a bead of water is coming up.
2. Check the battery cables to make sure they are tight and not frayed. The powdery stuff, the corrosion, should be cleaned off the cable ends and so should the terminals themselves. This is very important.

Sometimes a car is absolutely dead, you jump start it, and it starts right away. And you cannot understand what was wrong because the battery is not that old. Your problem could be a case of dirty battery cables. So be sure to check them.

Tools

One of the best reasons for being a do-it-yourselfer is that it gives you a good reason to collect tools. Whether you are a man or a woman, it is useful to have a good set of tools available for the right job at the right time (see chart on pages 137–138). For one of the great pleasures of life is deciding to do a job and having the satisfaction of knowing you have the right tool to do it. Conversely, nothing is more frustrating than planning to do something and discovering you do not have the needed tools.

When You Buy Tools Whether you do a lot of work on your car or just a little, get the best you can afford. Be careful about tools in those dollar bins you see in discount stores and supermarkets. In fact, be careful of anything you see in extremely low-price special sales. A 21-piece socket-wrench set for $9.95 will not last long. Five pliers for $5, or two wrenches for $1, if made of cheap metals, will not hold up and could damage what you are working on. It pays to buy a good grade of tool. Look for the Stanley, Craftsman, SK, KD, Snap-on—the best names in tools. Remember that you can justify the decision to buy almost any tool simply by calculating how much money you save by doing the job yourself.

Where should you buy your tools? Every supermarket, discount house, department store, hardware store, and auto-parts store has tools. The best bet is to find out what brand mechanics favor and what store carries them at the lowest prices. Do not buy el cheapos you have never heard of before.

Troubleshooting & Emergency Supplies for Your Car

Home Tool Box

allen wrench set	power sander
box-end wrench	rags
ignition wrenches	screwdrivers
hacksaw	socket-wrench set
needle-nose pliers	standard slip-joint pliers
open-end wrenches	water-pump pliers
power drill	wire cutters

Glove Compartment or Trunk

flares	gloves
flashlight	light-colored cloth
fuses	reflector
fuse puller	tire gauge

Emergency Tool Kit

aerosol drying spray	bottle of water
battery-cleaning tool	brake fluid

dry chemical extinguisher	pliers
electrical tape	plywood
ground cable for battery	power-steering fluid
ground cloth	radiator-hose tape
jack	screwdriver
jumper cables	small knife
hand cleaner	spare tire
lug nuts	taillight bulb
lug wrench	wheel chocks
oil (1 quart)	

Be extremely careful. Watch out for advertisements that promise a whole toolbox of "69 pieces for $39.95." The seller is counting everything but the rivets in the toolbox, and in addition to paying for the rivets in the toolbox, these sets often include tools you do not need.

What Tools?   If you are the kind of person who does things in a grand way and money is no object, buy that complete set of tools. Otherwise, go about it piece by piece. The logical place to start is with **open-end wrenches.** They come in a package, and if they are on sale, so much the better. Get a good set. They usually start at ¼" and then by increments of ¹⁄₁₆" go to ¾". These take care of most of your needs.

Next comes the socket-wrench set. If you buy it all at once you save money. Which size drive (or extension)? Ask if you are unsure, but you're best off starting off in the middle with the ⅜" drive, but you will want to purchase a ½" set later, this being a bigger, heavier set. A ¼" drive set can be handy for different jobs, but around a typical car or truck a ⅜" or a ½" is more like what you need. It gives more leverage, strength, and weight to work with. Once you have the socket set together, look at a metric set. Many cars and trucks come through today with metric parts, and a metric set could be useful. Once you have the basic socket set, regular and metric, look at a **box-end wrench set.** The box end differs from the open end in its construction. The open end looks like it has a set of jaws at the end. The box end usually has a circle at the end with a hole fitting over different sizes of nuts and bolts.

When you own different kinds of fixed-size wrenches, look for **adjustable wrenches**—a pair of **vice grips, standard slip joint pliers,** and **needle-nose pliers.** Later, when filling out the toolbox, add a pair of **water-pump pliers, wire cutters,** and a **hacksaw,** by which time you will discover a desire for a set of **ignition wrenches**—extremely handy to have when you are working on your car.

As for **screwdrivers,** you can buy them too good, but you cannot have too many. There is nothing quite as annoying as a cheap screwdriver that bends and twists when you use it. Paying $5 or $6 is excessive. There are good brand names that sell in the $2, $3, and $4 range that do not bend, twist, or break off at the ends. Pick screwdrivers up one at a time or in sets, but get good ones.

An **allen wrench** is sort of an inside-out wrench. Under normal circumstances, a socket fits down over a nut or bolt and all the other wrenches you use fit over a nut or bolt. An allen wrench works like a screwdriver—it fits into a bolt and becomes an interior twisting item that brings the bolt out. There are not many places where an allen screw is used, but running across one when you do not have the tool can be frustrating. Buy the full set so you have what you need when you need it.

Power Tools Everyone who works with tools eventually goes the power-tool route. They can be very expensive or quite cheap, or you can shop around for quality power tools somewhere between the two extremes. Unless you are going in for a complete home workshop—doing everything from an oil change to an engine rebuild—there are no power tools you *must* have. It certainly is good to have some, however, and the one you will get the most use from is the **power drill.** Almost everything you install on a car has a way of needing a hole drilled, and a good power drill makes this much simpler. There are also a variety of useful attachments for these drills. The handiest is a flexible rubber disk onto which you attach a circle of sandpaper. Grinding stones and wire brushes are good attachments that make many jobs easier than doing it by hand. A good **power sander** is a nice tool to have and is better than a disk attachment, which is hard to control. An orbital sander or a belt-powered sander is a fine tool to give that smooth finish when you are doing body work. You might also take a look at a saber saw, which cuts more exactly than most other saws.

Your Emergency Kit

I have given you a basic list of tools you need for your toolbox at home. Now, I want to cover emergency tools and supplies (see chart on pages 137–138). This is the equipment you should keep in your car or truck in case of that breakdown on the road. In the last chapter, I went over some of the equipment you should have in your glove and trunk compartments to take care of winter emergencies. What additional tools and spares should you carry year-round if you are the kind of person who likes to work on your own car? By working on your car, I do not mean doing a complete engine overhaul in the middle of an interstate highway—just those quick emergency repairs that will get you on your way without having to wait for a tow truck.

Flat tires are obviously the most common breakdown problem, and you should have a **jack** in the trunk of your car. It is worth spending $20 extra for a good jack, which is easier and much safer to use than the cheap one that came with your car. To change a tire efficiently, you also need a good **lug wrench,** a piece of **plywood** about 12″ × 12″ × ½″, and **wheel chocks,** wedges to place under the wheels to keep the car from rolling. And of course you should also have a good **spare tire** and a **tire gauge.**

In addition to tire and radiator supplies, there are some other items you should have in your car: an emergency light (costs from $2 to $20), flares, a reflector, a ground cloth, light work gloves, hand cleaner, and old rags. The emergency light will come in handy not just at night but also when you are trying to repair something in the dark recesses of the engine compartment. A flashlight may be good enough, but a light that will hang or sit squarely on a surface is easier. Flares and reflectors? Keep either or both—as long as you have something to place behind the car to warn motorists that you have pulled off to the side of the road. A ground cloth—a piece of plastic or a towel—is useful for changing tires and is certainly preferable to kneeling in dirt. The other supplies are self-explanatory—gloves or hand cleaner, so that when you arrive at your destination, you don't look as though you've been working on your car.

Why do I suggest a 12″ × 12″ × ½″ piece of plywood? The wood is to put under the jack in case you have to change a tire in mud or snow.

If you have mag wheels on your car but carry a standard spare tire, you will need an **extra set of lug nuts** that will fit that standard spare tire. Mag lug nuts are not going to fit on a standard spare.

Suppose you blow a radiator hose out in the middle of nowhere. You should have a replacement **radiator hose,** a **screwdriver,** a pair of **pliers, radiator-hose tape, electrical tape,** a **small knife,** and a bottle of **water.**

Make sure the hose is the correct one for your car. The clamps at the ends of radiator hose differ. One kind is the spring type you can remove with a pair of pliers, the other is the screw type, which requires the use of a screwdriver. The small knife you are carrying is used to slit the hose if it is stuck on the radiator outlet. The outlet is made of thin material and can be damaged if you try to twist off a stubborn hose. So make sure you have that knife.

Save the old plastic containers the coolant comes in, fill a couple with water, and put them in a remote corner of the trunk, tying them down so they do not roll around. Not only will you be able to replace your broken hose, but you can also put the water in the radiator at the same time.

By now you might think that your trunk compartment is supposed to be crammed with enough equipment to fit in the bed of a pickup truck. But we have more! In addition to tools and specific repair supplies, you should keep some **general spares** in your trunk, such as a headlight bulb, generally $3 or $4, a taillight bulb, 50¢ to $1, a ground cable for the battery, about $2 or $3, brake fluid, automatic-transmission fluid, power-steering fluid, and a quart or two of the kind of oil you use. Replacing the headlight will require using a **small screwdriver;** changing the taillight might necessitate removing the lens or replacing it from inside the trunk, depending on the type of car you have. Check and make sure you know how to do this before you buy the spare. Determine what tool is needed and add it to your list. Ground cables for batteries have a nasty habit of getting corroded and breaking. This doesn't happen often, but once is enough to make the precaution of keeping an extra on hand worthwhile, and it is certainly cheap. Carry some brake and transmission fluid. Although it will not cure a problem, it may be enough to get you where you are going so that you can have the problem cured.

8 Car Problems You Can Fix

1. The Engine Is Dead You turn the key and nothing happens. Something is definitely wrong, but what? Use the headlights to help you determine where your problem is. Turn the headlights on; if they don't go dim when you try to start again, the trouble may be with that neutral switch in your automatic transmission. Sometimes jiggling the lever in park or neutral while turning the key will help this problem. If your lights do go dim when you try to start, you could have a loose battery connection or corroded battery terminals. For either, loosen the bolts, carefully pry the clamps apart, lift the cables off, the negative side first, and clean those contacting surfaces until they are bright and shiny. Use a knife, emery cloth, screwdriver, or whatever you have on hand. Refasten the cables securely—the grounded or negative cable goes last—and attach them so firmly to the terminals that you can't turn them by hand.

If your lights still go dim you might have a low battery. If the lights do not go on at all your battery is probably dead or somehow disconnected, and you should try to solve that problem. Otherwise, you are going to need a jump start to drive to a service station or garage (see page 149). Always use caution when working around a battery.

2. The Car Refuses to Start In this situation, your engine does turn over and turns over fine, but it won't catch. There are three basic ingredients you are going to check: air, gasoline, spark plug. These three ingredients make the engine fire. And you are not getting fire.

If you have a strong gas smell, the car is probably flooded. Raise the hood. If you see gas on the engine, get professional help. If not, try cranking 10 seconds with the gas pedal pushed all the way down to the floor. Don't pump. If the car doesn't start, tap the carburetor lightly near the gas line, then repeat the entire procedure.

Now to find out about the spark. Remove one spark-plug wire. Twist and pull the boot off. Hold it by the boot, which is the rubber part that goes over the spark plug. Get a paper clip, twist it open, and stick one end inside that boot until it makes contact with the metal wire inside. Make sure the paper clip fits firmly into the end of the wire connector. Now, holding the *back end* of the boot with a rag, position the paper clip about an ⅛ inch from any nut or bolt on the engine. While someone else cranks the engine, watch for a spark.

If you don't see one, there is one other thing you can do. Pull out the short wire from the coil to the middle of the distributor and examine the ends. If you see corrosion, you need to try to get rid of it in (1) the hole in the coil, (2) the hole in the distributor, and (3) on the wire. Use emery paper, a file, anything handy to make that metal shine. Then put everything back together and again check for spark. Corrosion at one end or the other of that short wire can prevent you from getting spark or from getting enough spark at your spark plugs.

If you haven't found the answer yet, maybe your engine is not getting enough gasoline. If there is gas in the tank, remove the top of the air cleaner and see if the choke valve is stuck open. Push it shut and try to start the car. If that is not it, open the choke and look inside while someone pumps the gas pedal. If you can't see gas squirting, you've found the problem. And, unfortunately, you will probably have to get help. (This is one situation in which you should have a flashlight so you can look into those dark recesses.)

3. Overheating   If the temperature warning light on your dashboard goes red, what is wrong? Your engine is probably overheating. Pull off the road, turn on your flashers, and turn off the key.

Now open the hood to hunt for a water leak. It could be in the radiator itself or in the radiator and heater hoses. If you find a small leak in the hose, wait for the engine to cool and then tape it up. (If your tool kit has the equipment I have suggested, you will have hose tape!) If possible, loosen the radiator cap one notch to relieve the pressure. But be very careful or you will get burned. If the cap is hot, wait a while. After you have taped the leak and opened the radiator, drive *slowly* to the nearest gas station and get the leak taken care of. Don't drive around for any length of time with tape twisted around the radiator hose. If you have kept a gallon of water or coolant in the trunk of the car as I suggested, once the car cools down, take the radiator cap off and pour the water in. You will be able to drive much farther if you are prepared to refill your radiator.

No leak in sight? Check the fan belt. When you are missing a fan belt altogether because it broke somewhere on the road, you know that's the trouble, particularly if you have not found a leak in the radiator system. If you have a spare fan belt, you're set (see page 146). Otherwise, you can drive slowly until the warning light comes on again, stop, let the engine cool down, and drive slowly some more, repeating the process until you finally reach a place where you can have a new radiator fan belt put on.

4. A Wet Ignition Suppose you are on a highway, you drive through a deep puddle of water, and the ignition gets wet. What supplies should you have to take care of the problem? A screwdriver, an aerosol drying spray, and an old rag. Let's say you have driven through that puddle or the car has been sitting out in the rain and just will not start. The water is likely to be (1) inside the distributor cap, (2) on the spark-plug wires where they enter the cap, or (3) on the coil wire at either end, where it enters the cap or the coil. Using the screwdriver, remove the distributor cap, whether it is held down by screws or spring clamps, then wipe the moisture out of the inside of the cap. Wet wires can be dried with a rag or the quick and easy way with a can of drying spray, which is sold in many auto-parts stores. This is generally an electrically neutral fluid that sprays under pressure. It not only lubricates the metal and penetrates rust but also displaces water and allows electrical flow to resume.

It also might pay to pull that coil wire out at both ends, wipe it off carefully, and perhaps even use a little emery paper inside the female inlets. Get them free of corrosion and you may prevent ignition problems for a long time.

5. A Flat Tire The most common breakdown is a flat tire. I understand that most drivers know how to change a flat. Even if you know what to do, however, there are some rules and fine points that might not have occurred to you. So I will run through the whole process with you.

Step 1. That owner's manual I've mentioned is going to tell you exactly how to deal with your particular car's spare and jack. Park on level, solid ground. If you have an automatic transmission, put the car in park. If not, put it in gear. Always put the emergency brake on, too. If you have something to put in front of a wheel that will act as a wheel block, use it. Triangular wheel chocks would serve the purpose even better.

Step 2. Take the wheel cover off. Usually it will come off with a screwdriver or the tapered end of the lug wrench. Just pop it right off and, using the lug wrench, loosen each of the lug nuts one or two turns.

Step 3. Now, take that spare tire out. It is easier and safer to get it out before you jack the car up. Place the jack on solid ground, jack the car up. Again, the owner's manual will tell you where to place the jack and how to use it. You should get the flat tire at least 2 to 3 inches off the ground.

Step 4. Now finish removing the lug nuts, put them in the wheel cover so you can find them later, and pull off the flat tire.

Step 5. Put the spare tire on, tighten each lug nut snugly, but be careful not to jar the car off the jack while you are doing it.

Step 6. Bring the car down to level ground again and tighten those nuts one final turn. The final tightening should be done with the car back on the ground. First of all, it is easier, and, secondly, you do not take the chance of knocking the car off the jack. Do not tighten the nuts in sequence, but in a crisscross pattern. In other words, do not go in a clockwise or counter-clockwise direction around the wheel. Go crisscross, tightening the one to the bottom left, then the one to the top right, the one to the top left and, lastly, tighten the one to the bottom right.

Step 7. Do not put the wheel cover back on. Put it in your trunk with the flat tire. Every time you see the wheel without it, you will be reminded to get that flat fixed.

6. A Dead Battery The dead battery—how many times have you had that happen to you or your friends? For such an emergency, you need jumper cables. A good set is at least 12 feet long. Buy the flexible nontangling type, not the kind that bend like steel wire. You also need an adjustable wrench, a pair of pliers, and a battery-cleaning tool. These toolbox supplies cost only a couple of dollars and inevitably prove to be very helpful.

Jumper cables, also called booster cables, are an absolute must. They will enable you to render as well as to receive service. Turn to page 149 for the facts on safely jump starting your car.

But a dead battery may not be dead. It may have corrosion between the battery posts and the clamps on the end of the cable. Use the wrench to remove the clamps unless your car has spring clamps, in which case you need pliers. The cleaning tool has wire bristles that clean the mating surfaces of the battery posts and the clamp. Simply cleaning the contacts may eliminate the need for jumper cables, but keep them available anyway.

When you examine the cables, clamps, and all the rest, check very carefully whether the cables themselves are not corroded. Many so-called battery problems are nothing but cable problems.

7. The Fan Belt Snaps Suppose you are on the road and you throw a fan belt. If you have a well-equipped trunk compartment, you have a replacement belt, an adjustable wrench, and a screwdriver. When you buy the spare belt, though, make sure it fits your car. If the guy who sells it to you swears you are getting the right one, you will still have to check it yourself. You need a wrench to loosen up whatever it is the fan belt goes around—the alternator, power steering, air conditioner, and so on. This can usually be done with an adjustable wrench, but your car may need something other than this type of wrench. So, determine *in advance* what other type wrench you will need and put in your tool kit.

When you put the fan belt on and tighten up whatever you loosened, you will need something to pry with. You can usually do this with a big lug wrench, but, just in case, you ought to have a long, stout screwdriver, which is always a good addition to your tool kit.

8. A Fuse Blows If anything electrical fails—light, horn, radio—the first check should always be at the fuse box. Fuses can blow very easily, and you can replace them just as easily as long as you remember to keep a selection of fuses on hand in the glove compartment. Your owner's manual will tell you what each fuse controls, and most fuse boxes print the purpose of each fuse somewhere in the vicinity of each fuse. A fuse puller should be in everyone's glove compartment.

Breakdown Basics

If you have followed every maintenance suggestion in this book your car will probably never break down when it is being driven. Yet you ought to be prepared for the unexpected. Here are some things you absolutely must do when you get stuck—before you start to try to remedy the cause of the breakdown.

1. Get your car out of the way of traffic when it breaks down. If you have to flag down someone else to guide traffic while you push your car off to the side of the road, fine. But do not leave your car in the middle of the roadway—a surefire invitation to an accident.
2. Raise the hood, put on the emergency flashers, and tie a cloth to the door—preferably white, yellow, or some other visible color. If you have warning flares, and you really should, put one 10 feet in back of the car, one 300 feet behind the car, and a third flare about 100 feet in front of your car. Do not put the flare anywhere near spilled gasoline or the gas tank of your car.
3. The biggest question people ask me is "Should I leave the car to go for help?" That depends on where you are. If you are in a familiar neighborhood or a busy neighborhood and you know help is nearby, go for assistance if you need it. Otherwise, if you are in an unfamiliar or rough part of town, stay in your car and lock the doors. The raised hood, flashing lights and the white cloth are going to tell people that you need help. If other motorists do stop, roll the window down just enough to ask them to call for help. If they are really sincere, they will lend a hand. If they are not, they are still going to be locked out of your car.

Some people like to clean parts and tools with gas. Forget it. The most dangerous thing you can do is use gasoline as a cleaning fluid. There are plenty of cleaning fluids available at good auto-parts stores that will do the job cleaning parts and be a lot safer than gas.

Suppose, however, that you do have a gasoline fire. How do you extinguish it? Usually the best thing is to forget about fighting it, get everyone away, and call the fire department. But if you must fight the fire, do it properly. Above all, do not use water. It will only spread a gasoline fire. If you have sand, use it. Better yet, if you work on your own car, you should keep a **dry chemical extinguisher** on hand for emergencies—both gasoline and electrical fires. Most likely you will never need it, but if you do, it could save lives and money.

If you have gas in your garage, store it safely. Keep it in a container specifically for gasoline. These are generally marked "gasoline" and are usually red or orange, with a specific type of spout and specific safety precautions for use. Never store gas in plastic or open containers. If you must keep it around, keep it and use it properly.

The Exploding Battery

Yes, Virginia, batteries do explode, and they do so with mighty force. If you happen to be in the neighborhood, you can be seriously injured. When a battery explodes, battery acid splashes in all directions and pieces of the battery are blown in all directions. One cause of battery explosions is the spark that occurs when you connect jumper cables. The chemical reaction inside the battery produces an explosive mixture of hydrogen and oxygen, and under normal circumstances, this gas mixture escapes a little at a time and no harm is done. Sometimes, when a lot of this gas collects in and around the battery and something ignites it, you get an explosion. Vent caps on some batteries have flame arrestors, which prevent flames from the ignited gas from reaching the inside of the battery and blowing it apart. At this point, you may be thinking, "I do have to jump start the car occasionally. What should I do?"

How to Jump Start a Car

If you must jump start your car—that is, your battery is run down and you are going to use booster cables to borrow power from a good battery to start your car—it is important to understand that this procedure can be dangerous to you and harmful to the auto unless you do it properly. Most auto manuals include instructions for jump starting the vehicle. There is no universal procedure that applies safely to all cars. This is because some makes and models have special equipment or are provided with special battery hookups requiring a special jump-start procedure.

The first rule for jump starting is, Follow the directions in the owner's manual for that particular make. If you think I am overemphasizing this, don't bet on it! You can tear up an electrical system badly, even start a fire, or cause a bad explosion if you don't jump start the right way.

Before attaching the booster cables, make sure both the battery you are going to jump and the one you are jumping from have the same voltage—6 or 12 volts. Generally, this can be determined by the number of vent openings on the battery top. Six-volt batteries have three vent openings, 12-volt batteries have six.

Do you still think I am going into too much detail? Well, if you had seen what I have in the past couple of years you would realize that a warning on the dangers of jump starting is long overdue.

Both batteries should be clean. If they have caps on them, these should be removed.

Now you are ready to jump start your car. Position the two cars so the booster cables reach both batteries but do not allow the cars to touch. If the cars touch they will be grounded, and when there are certain differences in the wiring of the two vehicles, jump starting while they are touching can be hazardous.

Place the gear shift or gear selector of each car in park for automatic transmissions or neutral if you have manual transmissions.

Apply the parking brakes and turn off all accessories in both cars—radio, air conditioning, anything that draws electric power.

Never smoke around the batteries. Don't get sparks or flames near either battery while performing this process. Some owners have been injured jump starting their vehicles because of a careless electrical contact with rings, metal watchbands, and other jewelry. Be careful. If you don't take your rings and watch off, be sure you are exceptionally careful. In case of explosion, the use of protective glasses is also a wise precaution. And, of course, do not lean directly over the battery.

Tip: If you have a piece of wet cloth, put it over the battery you are jump starting. This will prevent splashing fluids or any gases that might come through from hurting you. Afterward, throw the cloth away. Don't play with it. Don't stick it in your pocket or do anything that could bring battery acid in contact with your skin.

Check the booster cables and vehicle batteries so that you can properly identify the cables' connection points. If the cables are twisted, separate them to avoid mistakes. Some booster cables are color coded and marked with a plus sign, the letter *P,* or "POS" for positive, and with a minus sign, the letter *N,* or "NEG" for a negative connection. Battery terminals are identified in exactly the same way.

Now connect one end of the positive booster cable, usually covered in red, to the positive terminal of one car and the other end of the positive cable to the positive terminal of the other car. Connect the negative booster cable, usually covered in black, to the negative battery terminal of the good battery. That leaves one final connection to make: the other end of the negative cable must be connected to the negative, or ground, connection on the car with the run-down battery. This final connection can be made at two points, and both choices involve an element of risk. And to make matters worse, there is a lot of disagreement about which is the better, safer procedure.

Method 1. Most motorists and service personnel connect the final battery cable, the final negative connection, to the dead battery; they will connect it to the negative battery terminal. Although thousands of cars have been jump started by making the last connection to the battery without incident, the possibility remains that the spark that results when you touch the booster cable to the dead battery can ignite battery gases. The possibility is considerably reduced, however, if you throw a damp cloth over all the battery caps or openings. Or if the battery has a flame-arrestor vent cap, or is the maintenance-free type that has no vent caps.

Method 2. The preferred method is to connect the final end of the negative booster cable to some point on the car frame, away from the battery. To the engine block or to some other good metallic ground.

If you don't know anything about your car, have someone else help you with this. In too many cases, drivers connect the other end to the carburetor or the cooling fan, both of which remedies are exceedingly dangerous. Ask a knowledgeable person to help if you are not sure of what you are doing. If you are sure, you are now ready to start the car. Make a final check to be sure all the cables are clear of fan blades, belts, and other moving parts. Be sure everyone is standing away from the car. Start the car with the good battery, wait a few minutes, and try to start the car with the discharged battery.

If the car with the bad battery does not start after cranking for 30 seconds, stop and check your procedures. One of the connections may not be solid. Go back to all four connections on the booster cables and gently rock them. Make sure the claws or teeth on the end of those cable connectors are grabbing solidly on clean metal. Make sure the area you grounded to, i.e., where you made the last connection, is free of rust or grease. Rock or shake the cables a little, see if you can get a better connection, and try once more. If at this point the car turns over very slowly, go back and rock the connections again while you let the other car run for a good 5 minutes. It could be that the dead battery was so deeply discharged that it won't start right away. Sometimes allowing the battery to charge for about 5 minutes will give you a shot at starting the dead car. If all this fails, if the car still does not start, get professional help. Something else is wrong. You need road service, a tow, and a professional to go into the car and find out exactly what the problem is.

Now let's assume the car starts. First, remove the negative booster cable from the last connection made to the car with the bad battery, then remove the positive cable, first disconnecting the end attached to the bad battery. In removing the cables be careful of all moving engine parts. Do not get your hands in the way of the fan. Remember, also, that you are holding two live wires that do not want to touch together. Keep them separated. Go back to the good car, that is, the car used as the booster, and remove those ends. Again, it is all-important that the cars don't touch, that the cables themselves are clean, that the connections made are clean, and that you do not touch those wires together when putting them on or taking them off.

FILL IT UP AND CHECK THE OIL

Chapter 10

THE GASOLINE DILEMMA

Once upon a time it was easy to choose a gasoline for your car. You pulled up to the station that offered the most green stamps and said, "Fill it up" with regular or high test. Today it's a different story, with low-test unleaded, low-test leaded, high-test unleaded, high-test leaded, and a number of variations in between. Octane numbers on the gas pumps have confused things even more, and most people today just try to find the cheapest gas that their car will stagger along on.

The worst part is that even when you go to the trouble of reading the owner's manual, and experimenting until you find the right octane number for your car, you find that as the car gets older, its gasoline needs seem to change. The villain in the piece turns out to be the federal government, which in its wisdom has decided that lead fouls the atmosphere and so has set out with the avowed intention eventually to end all use of leaded gasoline. Their reasons are pure. In many of our big cities, air pollution had reached the point where people were dying from it, and a large percentage of that pollution is caused by the automobile. The first attack on pollution was to remove the lead from gasoline and the second was to reduce all the other pollutants from a car's exhaust. In response, the auto manufacturers developed a thing called a catalytic converter, which chemically cleans up exhaust gases but cannot handle leaded gasoline at all. Whereas the original idea was to phase out leaded gasolines, the catalytic converter literally eliminated their use on most cars built from 1975 on.

Leaded vs. Unleaded

If you have a car made before 1975, you can use either leaded or unleaded gasolines, but the older the car is, the more likely it is to need at least some leaded gasoline every once in a while. This is because lead was used not only as an octane booster, but also acted as a lubricant for the valves. Although newer cars have specially hardened valve seats to make up for the lack of lubrication, older cars need at least one tankful of leaded gasoline out of every three or four to prevent excess wear. What this means is that if you have a problem finding leaded gasoline to run your car, you can live with unleaded. About 75% of the cars on the road will run on regular unleaded. For the older ones, get a tank of leaded once in a while when you can find it.

In choosing the unleaded gasoline you need for your car, the most important thing to remember is that premium costs a lot more than regular. If your car runs well on regular, or even on one of the lower-octane extra-cheap unleadeds, use it. The premium is only needed if your car pings or runs badly on the low-test stuff.

Sometimes it may pay to mix premium unleaded with low-test unleaded. This way you get a slightly more powerful gasoline than the low test, but you don't pay the high price of the premium for the whole tank. This requires some experimentation on your part to determine just what makes your car run best.

The Meaning of Octane

What are the octane numbers on gasolines? They are scientific measurements of the gasoline's ability to resist knocking, or pinging, as it's often called. That's the sound resembling a lot of marbles rattling around under the hood of your car, especially when you are accelerating up a hill, passing, or pulling out from a stop sign.

The octane numbers you hear about and see on the gas pump are actually obtained in the laboratory by running the gasolines in specially set up, 1-cylinder engines. I won't go through all the mathematics, but basically the engines are run first at a low speed under heavy load and then at normal speeds that simulate driving conditions when going up hills and the like. From these tests, the octane number is obtained and used to grade particular types of gasoline. Today, gasoline octanes range from 86 to about 93, with many gasolines available in between those numbers in both leaded and unleaded. I noted that you might find your car demanding different grades of gasoline as it gets older. This is because a certain amount of carbon builds up in your engine and actually increases the compression. The increased compression calls for higher octane gasoline. This is no problem if you use an 86- or 87-octane gasoline to begin with. You have a long way to go before you run out of higher octane blends. If, however, you are already using a 91 or 92 octane, and your car begins to ping, the best bet is to do something about the car rather than try to find higher-octane gasoline. And, luckily, you have several courses of action to choose from.

Two Cures for "Ping"

1. The easiest is to get the car out on the highway and while doing about 40 mph, floor the gas pedal, and keep it floored until you reach the 55 mph speed limit. Slow down and repeat two or three times. (By the way, since you are going to repeat this action a few times, you had best pick an uncrowded freeway at an off hour.) This should blow out most of the carbon buildup. Do not be surprised or upset if a black cloud of smoke comes out of your car.
2. If the car still pings, a stringent method must be used. The easiest is to have someone in the car rev up the engine to slightly above idle while you slowly pour about a pint of water through the carburetor. Yes, I do mean water. It will not harm the car, and it will knock the carbon out. If the engine begins to sputter as you pour the water through, back off until it catches again and then continue to pour. If you are afraid of water, do the same thing with one of the so-

157

called gas-treatment products that are for sale in the auto-parts stores. The biggest difference is that the gas-treatment products cost money.

Let's assume you have done everything above and the car still pings. Chances are you have a problem in the air-pollution control system, most likely in the exhaust gas-recirculation system. On General Motors cars and some others, there is an item called a thermal vacuum switch that can become stuck and cause pinging. In other cars, similar devices with other names can have the same effect. A thorough tuning of the air-pollution system is definitely in order if your car begins pinging for no apparent reason after having no problem when you first bought it.

Tip: The most important point to remember in choosing your octane is that you should use the lowest-powered gasoline that runs your car without pinging. Buying high test will not get you any better performance or mileage. The myth of more mileage from higher octane has hung on for many years, yet it's simply not true and you are just wasting your money.

Choosing the Right Gasoline

Is there any real difference in the various brands of gasoline? According to the gasoline companies, yes. There are 150 different hydrocarbons that can be used in various blends to make gasoline. Each company uses its own blend. They even change the blends in different seasons and in different parts of the country, particularly in high-altitude areas.

The average driver will never notice any difference winter or summer, high altitude or low, but the picky car owner may find it necessary to switch from one brand to another to get the standard of performance he or she demands in various seasons and different parts of the country. Some cars may respond better to one brand than to another because of the chemical makeup of the gasoline or the additives the company has used in its manufacture. Some gasolines even have special detergents to keep your fuel system clean; others have additives to absorb water that forms in the tank from condensation. Experimenting with various brands and grades of gasoline will ensure that you get just the right one for your car.

Quick Guide to the Right Motor Oil

Here is a look at everything you ever wanted to know about oil, and have been asking about quite regularly. Single grade, multigrade, petroleum base, synthetic additive, all synthetic—the chance of mix-ups in oils is astronomical today. Even when you walk into your local grocery store, they have a couple of different types of motor oil on the shelf. The question is what to use in your car, or truck. You may have read the owner's manual, noticed that it advised an SAE 10W40, API-rated SE, or perhaps an SAE 20W20, API-rated CD, and said to yourself, "Well, I'm not going to fool with all those numbers and letters." And you let the guy at the service station take care of it.

Not necessary! Your manual gives you those letters and numbers because every can of oil sold has numbers and letters like that on it. All you do is match up what the manual says to what's on the can.

So you won't be intimidated from now on, I'll give you some idea of what it all means. A 10W40, the most common type of oil, simply means that in cold weather, which is what 10W or "10 winter" stands for, the oil will be thin enough for your car to turn over easily. In warm weather, it will have a 40 consistency, or will be four times as thick, and that means that you will get the proper protection for the season. So much for the first set of numbers and letters. Your car probably uses a 10W40, an all-weather, multigrade, multipurpose motor oil. It is also a detergent motor oil, which means it has the added advantage of cleaning your engine. It is not to be mixed with nondetergents or single-grade motor oils.

If you use a 10W40 motor oil and it also says on the can "API-rated SE" or "SF," you are using about the best oil you can buy. If you have to add a quart somewhere down the line, what should you add? You should add exactly the same oil. If you can't get the same brand name, use a different brand, but it has to be a SAE 10W40, API-rated SE or SF. Regardless of what brand of oil the manual recommends, be sure the ratings on the can match what the manual says. Never mix differently rated oils, and especially do not mix a multigrade oil with a single-grade oil. Also avoid mixing a synthetic oil with a natural-petroleum product. If by any chance you do mix oils accidentally, drain the oil, change the filter, and put new oil in. Otherwise, you will gum up the oil pump and perhaps other parts of the engine. It is a mistake that can cause real damage.

Oil and Mileage   What about the new synthetic oils and the oils with additives that supposedly give extra mileage? They do work. You will get extra mileage from either the synthetics or the oils that claim extra mileage because of special additives. This works in two basic ways. (1) Some oils actually put a chemical into your engine that acts in the same way as millions of little ball bearings or slippery plates, causing your engine to run with less friction and therefore giving you better mileage. (2) Some oils add a chemical that joins with the metal parts of the engine, creating a new surface that is much more slippery.

There are several ways to improve fuel economy in our cars, and one is to reduce friction. Friction losses amount to approximately 5% of the energy you expend in the car in the form of gasoline when you run at full throttle, and when you drive in normal city traffic friction losses can increase to almost 50% of the actual energy that the car uses to run. Fifty percent! Which means that when we reduce friction, even a little bit, we get a lot better mileage. This is what the oil companies have set out to achieve with several types of products.

Some of the best mileage increases come from synthetic oils containing no petroleum at all. They are made up of chemical mixtures much more slippery than ordinary oil. A second type includes additives to ordinary oil, such as those chemicals that create millions of ball bearings which reach the moving parts in your engine and absorb friction. Both of these are known as "mechanical modifiers." The oil companies have also developed "chemical modifiers," which put special additives into your engine that actually coat engine parts and become part of the metal through a chemical change—like putting Teflon on a frying pan. When you add a chemical modifier, the engine parts don't stick together as much as they naturally do.

Both categories of product work to give you more mileage. They work so well that new car manufacturers are not allowed to use them in autos being tested for EPA ratings! Actually, the synthetic oils are so good the automobile manufacturers cannot use them because the engine would not break in properly. The oil is too slick and makes the engine run too easily for it to break in properly. This means that when you buy your car or truck from the dealer, the engine will have regular oil in it that should be left in for at least the first 5,000 to 7,000 miles in order to seal the rings properly and break in the engine. After that you can look to the synthetic oil.

Pros and Cons of Synthetic Oil   Synthetic oils have a tremendous temperature range. They pour nicely and lubricate well in temperatures ranging from –60®f to 450°F. To give you an idea of what this means, your normal oils would be like solid blocks of ice at –60°F and would actually become solid at heat approaching 500°F. Synthetic oils also have great strength and will hold to metal even under high pressures and heat. This means on many parts of your car where oil normally wears out, the synthetics hold up. They are better suited to extended periods between draining. You can leave them in the car longer because they don't oxidize or break down as fast as normal oils do. They reduce engine-oil consumption because of their low volitility and don't boil off. These are all fine features if your engine is in good condition. If you have an older engine with 60,000 or 70,000 miles on it, and have already developed a few creases here and there where oil drains through, you will find synthetic oils so slippery that they disappear on you and burn away simply because they get through all those little creases.

First among the general disadvantages of synthetics is the cost. Synthetics can cost two to three times the price of mineral oils but because they have an extended life you might conclude that they actually save money. Not true. Every oil has to be changed at least once or twice a year. Unless you put 20,000 or 25,000 miles a year on your car, synthetic oils could be very costly. You would do just as well with the petroleum-base oil.

Another possible problem is that many synthetic oils do not have nationwide availability. Remember, you don't mix synthetics, so if you needed a quart in a part of the country where the type that you had in the car is not sold, you would be in trouble. Also, synthetic oil should never be used in an engine that either burns oil due to mechanical problems—rings or valve guides—or in a motor that leaks. In either case, the engine would lose much more synthetic oil than it would mineral oil, and that loss would be expensive.

Lower oil-pressure readings can result from using low-viscosity synthetics, some engines might activate the oil-pressure warning light at idle. It doesn't mean that something is wrong with the engine, but it can be annoying.

Changing Oil Type If you decide to change the type of oil you use, you really ought to flush the engine. It is done by adding a quart of automatic-transmission fluid to the crankcase and running the car an hour or so at idle, after which you drain everything out and add your ncw typc of oil.

Never put yourself under a car held up by an ordinary bumper jack. When you put the car in the air, don't do it with a bumper jack. Put jackstands under any car when you change the oil, or use a roll-on ramp.

Buying Auto Parts

Beware! Those genuine parts you are buying may not be as genuine as you think. If you see a part for sale at a bargain price, examine it very carefully. Recently, auto-parts stores have been swamped with phony, failure-prone auto parts from places like Taiwan, Hong Kong, and Singapore. I will give you an idea of how this racket works. A company in England called Pioneer-Weston makes excellent automotive seals, and a new company, operating out of Taiwan, puts out a product called Weston seals. Not *Pioneer-*Weston, just Weston. The box is identical in color, shape, and everything else. The only difference is the slight change in the name. Or how about the counterfeit Lockheed parts that have been showing up? Counterfeit parts come in identical packages spelled L-O-K-H-E-E-D or L-O-K-H-H-E-A-D or L-O-O-K-H-E-E-D. And of course all these phonies bear the label of "genuine" on boxes identical to those the original parts come in. A similar gimmick is the parts box that has no name on it at all but is the same color or color scheme as a well-known brand. If you are not sure, ask to see the larger carton the smaller parts came out of to find out exactly who made them.

Choosing a Battery

Another major concern is the maintenance-free battery versus the conventional battery. Here are the facts. You can decide if you want to spend the additional dollars for the maintenance-free battery.

The conventional battery has a cell cap that you can remove periodically to check the fluid level. The water in these batteries tends to break down into gases, and occasionally you have to add more. That is why it has the cap. Water in such batteries breaks down because of high engine temperatures, particularly those produced by emissions controls on today's cars. If you do not replace the water when necessary, the battery can suffer permanent damage.

The maintenance-free battery uses different materials. Water loss is practically nil. Some maintenance-free batteries have the old-style removable caps, some do not. They all have greater resistance to damage from overcharging, yet they will not survive what is known as a "deep discharge." This means that if you run the starter so long that the battery goes totally dead, you may have lost one of these maintenance-free batteries. It cannot take that "deep discharge." A defective charging system or severe draining—draining to the point where the battery is almost dead—also ruins a maintenance-free battery. If you put it on the charger, however, it can be overcharged without too much damage.

Most batteries have a pro-rated warranty, so that just because you have a battery guaranteed for 60 months does not mean that in the fifty-eighth month the manufacturer will give you a new battery for free. What it means is that they will give you two months' worth of your money back.

Although hundreds of brand names are on the market, very few companies actually manufacture car batteries and usually the trade name is simply the distributor or the place selling it to you. They bought it from one of several battery manufacturers around the country. Thus, just look for the best warranties.

Putting a Car in Storage   I constantly get questions regarding the storage of an automobile. Son or daughter is going into the service or off to college. Or maybe you are planning a long trip without your car. Sooner or later nearly everyone decides to store his or her car. Perhaps it's a classic you want to save for posterity, or perhaps you're going to be away for a substantial period of time.

Generally speaking, unless your time away from the car is going to be more than 6 months, it does not require much in the way of special storage. Disconnect the battery, make sure all the fluid levels are proper, make sure there is plenty of air in the tires, and that's about it.

If you are going to be away more than 6 months there are some things you should do. First of all, take care of all normal mechanical maintenance. Change the oil and filters. Silicone brake fluid should be put in all the lines. Make sure the interior is clean and whatever protective coatings you use are properly applied. Wash the car and do touch-ups—polishing and waxing—and put an extra coat on all the exterior, particularly the chrome. Inflate the tires, and if you can, use bottled nitrogen gas to reduce oxidation of the rubber. If you cannot find it, live without it, but if your car is going to be up on blocks for any length of time, you can probably expect to lose some rubber. Run some white gas or aviation fuel through the carburetor. Then drain the fuel tank and the fuel lines.

Remove the spark plugs, put a little engine oil into the cylinders, and turn the engine over on the starter with the plugs out. This distributes the oil all along the cylinder walls. Having done that, replace the spark plugs. They do not have to be tightened fully, but they should be tight enough to make sure air or seepage do not get in. Last, remove the battery and store it.

Towing   A lot of people ask how well the new small cars can do towing. They want to make a trip with the travel camper they used with their old big car. Can they tow it with the new small car? They have seen on TV how a little truck can pull an entire diesel freight train.

Yes, on TV diesel freight trains are pulled by little trucks, at least for a short distance, but not for long. Not because the truck cannot pull the train—it can, just as your car might be capable of pulling a heavy trailer. Towing is not a matter of horsepower, it is a matter of cooling. Carrying a lot of weight is going to overheat your small car. Your owner's manual should tell you how much weight you can carry. Many companies put out weight-distributing hitches that enable small cars to carry a heavier-than-usual weight because all the weight does not sit on the hitch at the rear.

You should not take the chance of pulling more weight than the owner's manual calls for. Even with factory-installed heavy-duty cooling systems and heavy-duty springs and shocks, you will over-heat the car with too much weight. This is the one factor that limits how much you can tow. If all roads went on a straight line, there would not be a problem, but the slightest grade or hill will overheat a car that is pulling too much weight.

Load-distributing hitches are excellent, particularly for today's front-wheel-drive cars. The front-wheel-drive car gets all its traction from the front wheels. Putting a lot of weight on the back actually takes weight off the front, causing the car to get less traction. So, a weight distributing hitch is really needed for any towing job. But it does not give you the potential to carry any more weight than the owner's manual specifies. If you have a GM X body car, GM suggests 2,000 pounds for a trailer and that is all. Beyond that, the transmission cooler and the engine cooling system will fail, and you will destroy the car. Go on vacations, do your trailer towing, but stay within the limits of the auto.

Chapter 11

HOW TO HAVE THE SHINIEST CAR ON THE BLOCK

Let's take a look at the shine on your car. Or at the shine that you would like to be there. Today, all U.S. and foreign car makers use new acrylic lacquers and enamels, and they are better than those of just a few years ago. In fact, they have two or three times the durability and gloss retention of the earlier finishes. Nevertheless, no shine lasts by itself, and everybody wants a shiny car, polished to perfection and protected from rain and city dirt. The products on the market that maintain and improve car finish break down into several categories—rubbing compounds, polishing compounds, cleaners, cleaner waxes, and plain waxes. Along with these, you can purchase many specialized items for your car, including vinyl and chrome cleaners, fabric treatments, and even underside cleaners. There is also a new kind of product, the sealer lusterizer, usually designed to be applied professionally at a new-car dealership, although more and more do-it-yourself products of this type are appearing on the market. Professionally applied products run high—anywhere from $100 to $200, sometimes more—whereas do-it-yourself products cost from $5 to $40.

When it comes to caring for the car's exterior, though, paint gets the most attention. So let's start with those new sealer lusterizers.

This class of products has received a lot of publicity partially because of the high price tag and partially because of some manufacturers' claims that their product has extra molecular action, that it is like synthetic glass, that it bonds with the paint and provides an ultraviolet protective shield. Basically, these sealer lusterizers claim to protect the paint or eliminate waxing for years, and most of them have some kind of guarantee, some of which depend on following a regular maintenance schedule. Some brands offer a refund of the purchase price only for the product itself; others have limited warranties with no mileage or repair-cost limitations. A lot of claims have been made for them.

With dozens of sealer lusterizers on the market, there are far too many for us to look at each one individually. Instead, before you go out and buy a particular brand, consider the opinions of a few experts about these sealer lusterizers.

A senior engineer in charge of paint and corrosion systems at General Motors says, "We place them in the same general category as polishes and waxes. They make a nice-looking finish, but we haven't found any polish that preserves a car's finish." A technical manager of chemical products for Union Carbide believes that these products "do the same things as regular polishes and waxes." He points out that many of them require retreatment at regular intervals. "So, in effect," he adds, "you're repolishing the car regularly. If you do that with any good car polish, you'll maintain the car's good looks." The manager for coatings and systems at Chrysler thinks that "the widely advertised sealers and lusterizers do nothing to protect your finish."

As evidence, he cites long-term, side-by-side exposure tests made by GM and others in which identical production-line-painted panels were set out in parts of Florida where intense sunshine, high humidity, and salt air combined to make a very harsh environment. Treated and untreated samples were regularly checked for effects. *No differences were found.* That means that the protective value of these sealers is questionable.

However, sealer lusterizers do come up with a striking shine because of the plastic materials in them and perhaps because of the method of application, and many people are willing to pay the price for the immediate, good-looking result.

Should a dealer apply the sealer lusterizer or can you do it yourself? Many brands call for a preapplication of a mild abrasive compound and the use of a buffing wheel, which you are not likely to have at home. The dealer has the equipment and indeed its use is what puts the shine on the car. That is why dealer-applied finishes are often superior to do-it-yourself shines.

The problem with dealer applications is the cost, usually from $100 to $200, which may be more than you care to spend. But, if you like the idea, you can go out and do it yourself. Can you obtain the same results as a dealer without the same equipment? Well, with a little elbow grease you can. Before applying a sealer lusterizer, buy a light polishing compound, not a heavy compound. With a light polishing compound plus a little elbow grease your car will be ready for that sealer.

Waxes, Polishes, and Cleaners

How about the waxes, the ones you have used for years? You have probably waxed or polished with the more traditional products, which are often lumped together in a single category of waxes. Actually, there are five different types of products involved. The **rubbing compounds** are highly abrasive pastes for removing deep stains and scuff marks or for removing excess paint after a new paint job in a body shop. **Polishing compounds** are milder abrasive pastes for lighter stains and blemishes, for rubbing out spot paint repairs, or for preparing your car for a fancy wax job. **Cleaners** are liquids containing still finer abrasives and are intended for the removal of heavy dirt such as traffic film, insects, tree sap, and whatever else sticks to your car's exterior. Strictly speaking, rubbing and polishing compounds and cleaners belong in the polish category. **Cleaner waxes,** those familiar one-step products, contain both cleaner and wax and are fine for most jobs. Finally, there is **wax.** Car waxes are a combination of several different types of waxes and perhaps some silicone, and they must be applied to a freshly cleaned surface. Some require some elbow grease. Most classic-car and antique-car owners use good old-fashioned wax and elbow grease, the kind you have to rub real hard. But, boy does that wax shine!

Wax makes your car look good, as do polishes and cleaners. But experts agree that wax actually does little good for the car as far as protecting that paint job is concerned. Ultraviolet radiation from sunlight is the single biggest factor in the normal deterioration of automotive finishes, and nothing—whether it be a polymer, a wax, a silicone—nothing you can put on your car other than another coat of paint is going to protect the original coat of paint. It is impossible to measure what you finally leave on the car in the way of wax because it is such a thin coating. Anything that could truly stop ultraviolet light and the problems you have with your paint would have to be about ¼ inch thick!

Nor do waxes and polishes keep your paint from getting dirty or covered with road grime, although they do make this stuff easier to remove, and if you can keep your car clean, you are probably taking one of the best measures for extending the life of your car's finish. Washing stops deterioration, but do not get carried away. Too frequent washings can actually promote corrosion. One would think that washing would get rid of all the stuff that damages the car's finish, yet what washing really does is get a lot of water inside the body panels, which can create a problem on its own.

Going over the car every few months with a good automotive wax or polish removes the grime and detergent buildup. A couple of washings in between is really all you need. By the way, when I say a couple of washings in between, heading down to the local car wash is an error. Do it yourself. If the brushes are adjusted for a small or midsize car and you own a fullsize car, after a while the extra pressure will go right through your car's paint. In addition, some car washes use detergents that can be bad for the car. And the solvents in some of those so-called hot-wax processes can harm the vinyl top. In other words, wash your car yourself. Washing only takes a few minutes, and if you do it the right way (see page 171), it makes the car last longer. It's nice exercise, too.

Now, if reading the foregoing has made you decide it is time to wax your car, almost any good automotive wax or cleaner will do the job properly. What if you own a used car? Well, if the finish is in good shape, treat it just like a new car. A dry wax with a high concentration of polishing abrasives, a so-called cleaner wax, should work. If that does not do the job, try a polishing compound. If all else fails use a rubbing compound. Be a little careful when you use heavy rubbing compound, however, because it can easily go right through the paint.

Protecting the Vinyl Roof

Oh! Those vinyl tops! They really require some special precautions. Under normal conditions, the most important thing for your vinyl top is to keep it clean with washing, although like the paint, it has to be cared for in other ways, too. But the one thing you never do is wax it. Nearly all car waxes and polishes contain abrasives that will damage the thin coating of clear acrylic covering the vinyl top and giving it its shine. Use only vinyl-compatible cleaners and treatments. Do not go near a vinyl top with any household solvent or cleaner. The vinyl top requires its own polishes, its own waxes, and whatever you buy must specify "for vinyl roofs" on the container.

The Interior

If you have a vinyl interior, everything that has been said about vinyl tops goes for the vinyl interior. Experts say that they see no reason to treat leather or vinyl interiors, both extremely resistant to stains and soils, with stain repellents or similar products. However, there are some good stain repellents for cloth interiors. The products that you use for your draperies or couch will do. If you can find an automotive brand that sells for the same price as the household soil repellents, fine. Sometimes, automotive salespeople think they can charge a little extra because the product has the word "automobile" in the title. But since there is really no difference between stain repellents for interior upholstery and ordinary home products, do not pay extra money just because it says "automobile" on it.

I recommend avoiding those quick car washes as well as the do-it-yourself car washes. Again, harsh soaps dry out the paint, and a direct stream of high-pressure water will drive dirt particles right into the paint, making things worse than they ever were. Having given you two ways *not* to wash a car, here are two methods that will not hurt your car's finish.

Method 1. The normal way to wash your car is to use a hose spouting cold, clear water and gently rinse the car. Start with the top, then the hood, sides, front and rear. Do the rocker panels and the wheels last. Flood the dirt off with a spray—do not drive it in with a direct blast. Now fill a bucket of water and soak a clean Turkish towel with a nice deep nap in the bucket, sloshing any remaining dirt off the car, stopping to rinse the towel after every slosh. Start at the top and work down, finishing with the rocker panels and the wheels. Rinse the car once more with a gentle flood of water from the hose. When you are sure that it is clean, dry the car thoroughly, again using a clean Turkish towel. That is the first and most common way.

Method 2. A better way to wash your car is a little more work, but worth it. This is called the "three-towel" method, and it has the added advantage of using only two or three gallons of water so you can do it almost anywhere with very little mess.

1. Start with a bucket of clear, cold water and three Turkish towels with a deep nap. Put the first towel in the bucket, slosh it gently over the first section of the car starting with half of the top. Rinse the towel after every slosh.
2. When all the dirt has been sloshed off, use your second towel to wipe off the surface. It will soon become damp so you will get the car only partially dry.
3. Then take the third towel and use it to wipe the car totally dry.

Follow those same three steps on the other half of the top, each

half of the hood, and so on. You will wind up with a clean car.
Notice that in neither method did you use soap!

Rust—Enemy Number One

Time for a look at the age-old problem with the auto—rust, a problem that eats away millions of dollars' worth of automobiles every single day. While there are thousands of cars on the road 10 to 15 years old and still giving good service, many others less than 10 years old wind up in junkyards. Victims of rust. Rust is the prime enemy of the automobile. Between the two extremes of the car in the junkyard and the car running 15 or 20 years are varying degrees of automotive structural decay of which some examples are just unsightly and some actually make holes in body work.

Undoubtedly, you have seen quarter panels rusted out, rust around rear and front windows and at the bottoms of doors. In many cases, rust causes structural damage to frames and undercarriages, making a car unsafe without the owner's even being aware of it. Any car can rust. Rust has shortened the lives of hundreds of thousands of vehicles and has cost owners millions of dollars. Yet rust can be prevented.

First, however, let's think about what rust is. In scientific terms, rust is the oxidation of metal from its exposure to air and water. That process can be speeded up by corrosive substances on the road or in the air. The more obvious and less serious result is unsightly deterioration of the body of a car, but some results of rust are far more serious—for example, the weakening of the areas under floor mats and carpeting, of the third-seat area in station wagons, and of the frame and cross members. The problem is prevalent in many areas of the country, but particularly where the moisture in the air contains salt as well as in areas where salt is used on the roads during winter. Salt, calcium chloride, and other chemicals used on icy roads are corrosives that take their toll on the undersides of automobiles.

Before buying a used car, examine it carefully for rust. Look at the body and underside, frame and cross members. Be alert for signs of repainting and body putty that attempt to disguise any area where rust has already done damage. Pay attention to doors, fenders, quarter panels, rear windows. If the used car is a station wagon, take out the spare tire, examine the tire wall, and lift up the mat on the floor in the area by the third seat to check for rust and weakening of the metal. The backs of station wagons are a particular problem. In other cars, lift up the mat in the trunk and the carpeting in the passenger area if you can. Be suspicious if the car smells musty. That could be a very dangerous sign.

Antirust Maintenance You must start your rust-prevention program the day you buy your automobile. You can't wait until you see rust, you have to beat it before it happens. To prevent rust, keep your car clean, wash it frequently, and wax it at least twice a year. Hose down the underside at least twice a year, too, particularly if you live in an area where sand and salt are used on the road. When is the best time? Midway through winter and at winter's end. Use a little extra effort to wash out the inside channels of the frame or cross-member components, and clean out accumulated leaves and other debris that retain moisture. Keep the drain holes in the frame, floors, and bottoms of the doors free.

Tip: Here is a little trick to use in washing and keeping the underside of your car clean. You have seen those hoses with the holes that you use on the lawn. You spread them out, and they fire water in all different directions. On a dry day, when your car will dry properly, lay one of these hoses out on your driveway and run your car back and forth over it, moving the hose occasionally so you reach the different parts of the car. Make sure the water pressure is strong enough to blow out the grit, grime, salt, and anything else caked on the underside.

Occasionally get your car up on a lift. Check to see that the undercoating is working properly, that it isn't cracked and chipped and allowing rust to form. Make sure all the drain holes in the bottom of the car doors are kept open, and after you have washed your car, leave the doors ajar for a few minutes to permit all the water to drain out from your washing. It is bad enough that water gets in the door panels in the rain. Most people do not realize that when you wash a car the same thing happens, and that you need to make sure that water doesn't stay in there.

After driving in heavy snow or slush, where the car is exposed to sand and salt thrown, by passing vehicles, wash the car as soon as possible. A white film on your car from winter driving is a positive sign of salt from road splash. Wash it off at once. Inspect your car periodically, particularly after a snowfall. If you notice any extreme weakness or deterioration of the structural members, rusted out portions of frames or cross members, have a welding shop strengthen the weakness.

At the first sign of any rust spots, have them cleaned and repainted. Lift the mat in the trunk regularly and look for rust there. Also inspect the areas around body molding, fenders, and body scrapes. Take care of even a slight bit of rust. Any bubbling under the paint means rust—get it taken care of.

Rustproofing At the time you purchase your vehicle, consider having it professionally rustproofed at the dealer or by an establishment that specializes in such services. It is not a cure-all but it is somewhat of a preventive.

People think that undercoating takes care of rustproofing, but rustproofing cannot stop with mere undercoating. Undercoating, if applied properly, provides some measure of protection, but it is no guarantee against corrosion. It can crack and flake off, leaving portions of the car unprotected or allowing moisture to enter cracks. A professional rustproofing involves treatment of all vulnerable areas—insides of the doors, rocker panels, and the like. A good rustproofing job means drilling holes in some spots in the body of the car in order to shoot in a waxy petroleum product that coats the area and keeps rust from getting started inside.

Undercoating When you decide to have your vehicle undercoated, have it done before taking delivery. It is too late to take the car back for undercoating after driving it for a week or two and acquiring a buildup of dirt. Undercoating at this stage is not what it could be. A proper undercoating involves coating of all sheet-metal surfaces under the car. The gas tank, exhaust system, and areas around the catalytic converter should not be undercoated—people who smell oil in their new cars often have a car that someone mistakenly undercoated in one of these places. Make sure the people who do the job know what they are doing so they cover the right places.

Undercoating is not perfect protection. You have to keep a watch on it, yet it does extend the life of your car, and the new rubberized undercoatings are proving to be much better than the old tarlike substances.

Does Your Car Leak?   You have taken delivery of your rustproofed and undercoated car from the dealer, and now you are going to find out whether the car has a leak that can cause problems. *This is the only time to take your car through a car wash.* Car washes are not good as far as the finish of your car is concerned, but they can help you find leaks because they spray water at you from every possible direction. Look for leaks around the windows and doors. If you see any, take the car back to the dealer and have them corrected immediately. Make sure you try to see exactly where the water is coming in and write down your observations. Sometimes when you see water dripping from under the dashboard the leak is tough to find. Usually, that sort of leak comes from the windshield area, and the windshield needs to be resealed.

Don't overlook the possibility of leaks from below. Spray the underside and wheel wells with a hose. Use a forceful spray to make certain there are no openings that permit water to enter and remain under floor mats or carpeting. If you see spots where water is coming in, caulk the openings. Do this yourself or, again, go back to the dealer. Many sealing products on the market work, and any good auto-parts store can tell you what to use.

After you have looked over a used car that you like, do the same thing I suggest doing with a new car. Drive it through a car wash to check for leaks. The owner of the car, whether it be a used-car lot or a private owner, can't object to your taking it through a car wash, and you will find out if it has leaks.

Chapter 12

GET YOUR HANDS OFF MY CAR!

Many people believe that if a thief wants their car, they can do nothing about it. Well, that is wrong. According to the FBI, most cars are still stolen by amateurs, and they are stolen because they are easy to steal. Eighty percent of all stolen cars were unlocked, and 40% actually had the keys in the ignition. The most important step you can take, obviously, is to lock the car and pocket the keys. Most amateurs will not bother breaking in. It is easier to shop for an unlocked car with the keys in it.

You may ask "Why would anyone steal my car? It's nothing special." The fact of the matter is that a car need not be new, nor does it have to be a fancy model to be something that somebody wants. Thieves may want it just for salable parts. Or they may want it because they have one like it that they can paint over and redo using your car's identification numbers. Even though your car is ordinary, the professional thief could have an eye on it. Car theft is a multibillion dollar industry, and car-theft rings go after old cars, new cars, any cars they can make a buck on. Today, most of those cars are gone in less than 2 hours after they are stolen. When I say "gone," I mean stripped down to the bare frame. The engine is gone, the transmission is gone, every important part is gone. A good chop-shop can take your car apart in about 20 minutes. Twenty minutes—from a car that runs to a hundred pieces scattered around the floor to be shipped out to various salvage yards and body shops.

Certain cars are almost always the object of a thief's attention. First, Corvettes, second, Cadillacs, and third, any car that is extremely popular, such as Mazda RX7, Datsun 280ZX, and the like. These are the cars that are being stolen. Their parts are expensive and somebody who can steal one and strip the parts off and sell them will come up with a bundle of money. It is far more profitable these days to sell cars for parts than to sell the entire vehicle. This fact has caused the stolen car business to change radically over the last few years.

Putting Off Car Thieves

How can you protect your car against car thieves? Here are some suggestions from the Boston Police Crime Prevention unit. Boston, by the way, was at one time the car-theft capital of the world. In the corridor between Boston and New York, more cars were stolen than along the entire East Coast.

• First of all, roll the windows up tight. Store the spare keys in your wallet, not in your car. Believe me, every professional knows all the hiding places you can think of. Those little magnetic boxes that you conceal under the fender or under the hood are the first things he looks for.
• Replace those standard door-lock buttons with slim, tapered door lock buttons. You have seen them in auto-parts stores. They are almost impossible to pull up with a bent coat hanger or a piece of wire—the most common thieves' tool.
• If you keep your car in your driveway, park it with the front toward the street. That means that anyone who raises your hood and starts to fool with your engine in an effort to start it will be seen from the street and, with luck, by your neighbors.
• No matter how short your errand is, do not leave your car running outside a store or even in your own driveway. Many amateur thieves hang out at convenience stores and other parking lots waiting for just such an opportunity.

• Install different locks for the door, ignition, and trunk. This means you are going to be carrying three keys around: one to open the door, one to work the ignition, and a third to work the trunk. The key that opens the door will not work the trunk or the ignition. An attendant in a parking lot who uses your ignition key cannot use it on the trunk.

The basic idea is to make stealing your car time-consuming. If it takes a long time to get to, the thief will most likely give up and try his luck on someone else's car. That means that everything that can be locked is locked. Make sure the windows are rolled up tightly, and if possible, turn your wheels toward the curb so that if the culprit tries to push your car away it will not go anywhere.

Tip: If you do park in a lot quite often, leave only the ignition key. Parking lots claim no responsibility for anything stolen from the trunks of cars, so do not let anyone get at yours.

Antitheft Devices

Do antitheft devices really work? Many of them do, and some are good enough to get discounts from insurance companies in some cities. What devices have proven effective? The amateur thief can be foiled by almost anything. The professional, however, is another story. Here are five products designed to protect cars from the pros.

1. The **kill switch** is like having a second ignition switch. Your car will not start unless a hidden switch is activated. When you install one of these, you have to get the ignition key turned on and throw a second switch in order to start the car. Taking time to find out where you have hidden the switch could be more than even the professional thief wants to deal with.
2. An **alarm system** consists of a loud warning sound that signals an alert when the car is tampered with or jostled. This device, however, has one problem—if someone bumps the car in a parking lot or happens to lean on it, the alarm could go off. I have known some to go off in a high wind, which could present a problem if that happens during a

storm at 3 o'clock in the morning in your apartment-complex parking lot. This antitheft device works, but it can be annoying.

3. A **fuel-switch device** is a protective measure that works by closing a valve that regulates the fuel supply. The thief who gets your car started will suddenly run out of gas about a block away. The switch is usually hidden under the seats or in other hard-to-find spots.

4. The **armored collar** is a metal shield that locks around the steering column and covers the ignition. Supposedly, it keeps even someone with a key from getting to the ignition switch and starting your car.

5. The so-called **crook-lock** is a bar that locks the steering wheel to the brake pedal. Generally speaking, however, this device is less effective than some of the others.

6. If you park on the street, look for a spot that is well lighted and heavily trafficked at night. Plan ahead during the day. Consider buying **special locks for easy-to-steal parts** like the wheels, gas caps, and seats, and a **hood lock** to protect the engine and battery, and other inside parts. A hood lock can prevent a thief from disabling antitheft devices with wiring behind the dashboard.

Antitheft devices can cost anywhere from $10 to $300. If you do buy one, let an expert install it. Do-it-yourself jobs are usually easier to defeat. When you buy a new car check the manufacturer's list of antitheft devices. Virtually every company now has a range of options. Be aware, however, that if the antitheft device is factory-installed, the factory alerts the repossessors of the location of the device and how to disarm it. If the repossessor knows, it's only a short while until the thieves know.

Professional thieves usually change the identification number on stolen cars, so what you should do is mark your car in several hard-to-find spots. For instance, mark the engine or body or, easiest of all, drop a business card down the slot between the door and the window. That way, if you see a car that looks like yours, you can call a cop and say, "If it is mine, the business card will be. . . ."

Get yourself an **etching tool.** In most stores, these cost only $10 to $15 or maybe a little more. Etch the vehicle identification number on the side windows and on every place with some metal that can be seen but will not really hurt the looks of the car. Etch that vehicle number on the base of the seats, on the steering wheel, somewhere on the dashboard and in the glove compartment. When a thief sees those identification numbers etched on the windows, he realizes immediately that you have attempted to protect your car and may think twice.

Some people customize their cars with pinstriping or unusual body paint. When stolen, they are harder to dispose of and easier for police to spot. But **customizing** does not help you when thieves are after only parts. Parts can be disguised very quickly. Auto strippers can strip a car naked right where it is parked and do so in about 20 minutes. When I say naked I mean that they do not leave anything but a frame or the few body parts that they would have to cut out with a welding torch.

Do you know your license plate number? Do you check the plates regularly? If a thief steals your license plates to put on a hot car, the stolen plates are likely to end up on your car, and that could be very embarrassing when the police stop you.

How do you keep your car safe in a parking lot? Do not tell the attendant how long you are going to be unless you must. Leave only the ignition key, as I mentioned. Write down your odometer and fuel-gauge readings on your claim check, in the view of the attendant if possible, and check those readings upon your return to make sure that no one has driven your car, switched its parts, or perhaps even committed a crime with it. (These things *do* happen.) Take the claim check with you and, ideally, your car keys. Most importantly, never leave that claim check in the car or someone else may drive away with it. Luggage, packages, purses, and anything sitting in the car are begging to be ripped off. Take the trouble to lock them in the trunk.

Tip: If you are on vacation in another state, your out-of-state license plates are always a dead giveaway that the trunk is full of valuables. So, when you stop at night, unload the car.

Chapter 13

DRIVING TO AVOID ACCIDENTS AND WHAT TO DO IF YOU HAVE ONE

Defensive Driving

      The secret of defensive driving is to assume that the other guy is not going to do it right; that the other guy doesn't know the law and doesn't know how to drive. This is not an unwise assumption when you consider what happens on the road today. Always assume that other drivers know nothing about driving and got their licenses by mail order.

"Defensive driving" means driving at all times with an awareness of two important rules. Rule #1: You never have the right of way. Rule #2: On a clear stretch of road with no cars in sight and no intersecting roads, something will fall out of the sky and land on you. Together, the two rules mean, Be ready for the worst.

According to the first rule, when you are approaching an intersection, you are approaching the most dangerous situation in driving. A third of all accidents occur at intersections. *There is no right of way.* The fact that the law is on your side will not stop an idiot from plowing into you broadside. The existence of stop signs at an intersection will not prevent an idiot from turning onto or crossing the road and smashing into you. *There is no right of way.*

Just because the law says you are allowed to go freely through an intersection doesn't mean other drivers will agree. Before proceeding through any intersection, whether you have what you think is the right of way or not, look first to the left, then to the right, then back to the left again. Turn your head when you look. Really look. A quick glance is not enough.

There is a point at which you must decide to stop before you reach the intersection or proceed through it. At 30 mph, that point is 90 feet from the intersection. That's a long way. On a residential street that means you make your decision about halfway through the yard of the second house from the corner, the average front yard being about 60 feet wide.

Even if the law gives you the right of way, take your foot off the gas when you reach the second house before the intersection. Then you can stop in time if you have to.

Always slow down at intersections because the guy coming in the other direction may not.

You also might run into unidentified flying objects on the road. Baseballs, Frisbees, kites, even a bee flying through your window. Be ready to stop your car. A kid usually follows that Frisbee, or ball, or kite.

Is a parked car a hazard to you when you drive? You're driving down a normal residential street, cars are parked on one or both sides. No one is moving, everything is fine. No one threw a baseball into the street, nobody threw a Frisbee through your window, no bees have come in to sting you. Is danger lurking in this situation? You bet it is. To be ready for it, you must check every parked car from behind as you approach it. Look at the steering wheel. If you see a person sitting behind that wheel, assume that he or she is going to pull out in front of you or into you. Whenever you see someone behind the wheel of a parked car, take your foot off the gas and be ready to brake and turn. Expect that person to pick the moment you are driving by to start the car and cut right out into the middle of the road. Parked cars are always a hazard.

Even when you are in front and the other guy is behind you, you can get into trouble. Rear-end collisions are very dangerous. When you realize that you are going to slow down, or hit the brakes rapidly, or even stop, tap that brake pedal a couple of times to warn the idiot behind you. It may do no good, but at least you have given some warning. If you don't, he or she will surely be climbing up your trunk compartment. What if you must make a panic stop and don't have time to blink your brake lights at the car behind you? The best driving technique is to avoid putting yourself in such a situation by being careful and watching ahead all the time. Always maintain at least a 2-second following distance, keep your eyes moving to spot potential hazards before they reach the panic stage. If you see children playing along the side of the road, slow down; you never know when they are going to run out in front of your car.

Curves are one of the most hazardous areas on any road. On many roads, a left-hand curve or a right-hand curve is so sharp that it becomes blind to you right beyond the bend. On a two-lane highway, the right-hand curves are more hazardous. More right-hand curves tend to be blind because of trees, hedges, or fences close to the shoulder. These can obstruct your view of the oncoming traffic. If you don't reduce your speed enough to take a right-hand curve, your car can be forced into the path of vehicles coming at you the other way. With the left-hand curve you are on the outside, and if you do tend to lose control at least you will go off the road and not into the path of another car.

Freeways have many hazardous situations. Lane changing probably causes more freeway accidents than any other maneuver. If you see another vehicle changing lanes or if a vehicle is in a position where it might change lanes, stay away from it.

Glance at the outside mirror, at the cars or the trucks in the lanes next to you. If you can't see the driver's face in your mirror, then you are in his or her blind spot. That person cannot see your car. Either move ahead or drop back so the driver can see you. Unfortunately, that blind spot is right off the driver's rear fender. More accidents are caused with two cars that are close together, one right off the rear fender of the other, than any other position on the highway. If you are passing someone on the right, be sure the other driver sees you.

Always use your signals when you are passing on a freeway. Whether entering, exiting, or changing lanes, signal your move in plenty of time for the drivers around you to see what you are going to do. It may not do any good, they may ignore you completely, but at least give them a chance to pay attention.

When a vehicle has passed you, especially a long 18-wheeler or someone pulling a vacation trailer, flick your headlights up and down. This signals the passing driver that it is safe to come back over into the right lane. Many truckers say "thank you" with a blink of their lights. If you don't signal, the passing vehicle might come over too soon. Even if you do signal, be on the alert.

In downtown traffic, exits to parking garages or truck-loading docks in the middle of a block become hidden intersections. When you spot a gap in a row of parked cars, with luck you have found a parking space, but it could be a driveway. Somebody could be on the way out, and you should watch carefully.

An exit sign sometimes warns you of cars leaving a parking lot. But not always. Anytime you see a sign that says "parking," be aware that a car might be coming out right at you as you go by. Some garages and loading docks mount a large mirror near the sidewalk to tip you off to the possibility of cars or trucks coming out.

How about the right of way you are sure is yours—the green light? Green light. That means "Okay, go ahead." Right? Wrong. When you have a green light, you probably proceed through the intersection and assume the cross-street traffic will stop and stay stopped. If so, your assumption can be wrong. You must protect yourself from the guy who tries to make the yellow light, the driver who doesn't care whether the light is green, red, or yellow. When your light has just changed to green, remember, look left, look right, look left. *Turn your head* when you look. Make certain the way is clear before you move.

When approaching a green light, if you are interested in driving defensively, you are going to look left, right, and left again. Before you reach the intersection. If you are making a right turn on red, look for the movement of other cars. By the same token, when you are moving on green, look out for the driver making that right turn on red.

Remember, you never have the right of way definitively because any idiot can take it away from you in an instant.

If an Accident Happens

What do you do if you are involved in or see an automobile accident? Both the law and ordinary human obligations are involved. The most important things to remember when a serious accident occurs are:

1. Don't panic. Keep your wits about you and think. What has to be done? What should you do first? Second? Third? Plan what to do in a logical order.
2. If you have to administer first aid, don't do more than you are capable of doing. Make sure qualified people get to the scene to give first aid, to give help, to do what is needed.
3. Stay on the scene, or you can be charged with leaving the scene of an accident.

Being involved in an accident does not necessarily mean you or your car were physically struck by another vehicle. If you are double parked and a car swerves to avoid you and hits someone else, you are involved in that accident. If two cars collide trying to avoid your car in any manner, you are involved in that accident. Do not leave the scene. If you pass someone and his or her car runs off the road because of it, you are involved.

There is another situation in which you are expected to render aid. If you are the first to arrive at a bad accident, you should do certain things. No law dictates that you have to do them, but human consideration comes into play.

1. Avoid a second collision—don't park behind the wreck or on the opposite side of the road. Pull up several yards beyond the accident and turn on your flashers.
2. If it is safe to do so, reduce any chance of fire by turning off the ignition in the crashed car if someone has not already done so.
3. Assist the injured people, ask where they are hurt. Check to see if someone is not breathing. Look for severe bleeding. Do not play doctor, however. You don't know how, unless you really are a doctor. Do not move accident victims unless it is absolutely necessary. There could be a neck or spine injury, and moving the victims could prove fatal. In the exceptional case when a car is burning or another imminent danger threatens that car, then you might carefully move the victims.
4. If there is smoke coming from the wreck, look at it carefully. It could be steam from the radiator and not smoke

from a fire. Don't panic and figure smoke means a fire until you have made sure it is not just a broken radiator.

5. Get help. Radio or phone the police or ambulance, fire department—anyone you can think of. If you are busy giving first aid, ask others to stop to warn off approaching traffic. Use flares and reflectors where possible.

6. Search the area for victims who might have been thrown from the cars.

What should you do when you are involved in an accident? You are legally bound to stop whenever you are involved in an accident. You must stop, identify yourself, and aid the injured, if possible. Stop as close to the scene as possible, yet try to get your car out of the flow of traffic. Make sure you note the location in order to draw up the proper traffic-accident report. Make sure you have in your mind or down on paper an idea of exactly how the cars were placed and how the accident occurred. You will need it later. Under many circumstances, you will have to notify your insurance company as well as the police, and will be required to file an accident report. You should really keep a blank accident report form with you. Many insurance companies provide them with the policy when you join up. Otherwise, be sure to get one from the police.

You are allowed to direct traffic around an accident even though you are not a policeman. Do so until the police arrive. One important factor—position yourself in such a way that you can get out of the way in the event that an uncooperative driver comes along and decides he or she is not going to obey your signals because you are not in uniform. Be ready to jump to the side of the road.

Lastly, you should know some basic first-aid procedures. It is essential to know how to stop bleeding, which is the most important thing a layperson can do to help an accident victim. To be truly prepared, keep a first-aid kit in your car.

GOOD-BYE, OLD FRIEND—WE COMPLETE THE 100,000-MILE CIRCLE

Chapter 14

THE OLD CAR—TRADE OR SELL?

When it comes right down to it, the biggest problem you face while buying a new car is how much will you get for the old one when you go to buy the new one? When it comes to the choice between trading your car for something better or selling it privately, there is very little evidence to support the trade-in. Actually, most people trade their cars because it's the convenient way to do it—the old car becomes part of the down payment.

Car dealers are professionals (I have said this before), and they make a margin of profit on every unit. It is understandable that they are going to give you fewer dollars than a private individual. Dealers have absolutely no emotion about the cars they buy and sell. You may love your 1962 squareback V-8 whatever, but to the dealer it has no more significance than a can of dog food. The dealer gets market advice every day from the blue book, the red book, the banks, wholesalers, insurance contacts, and his or her intuition, whereas all you have is your love for your car and a few newspaper ads to show what it is selling for elsewhere. The problem with that love affair with your car is that it is almost over. You have found something newer, better, and shinier and thus are likely just to drop your car off at the dealer and take whatever is offered for it.

You would probably be better off if you did what the dealer intends to do with your used car. Touch it up a little bit, spend a hundred dollars, get it in top shape, and then sell directly to someone. You will probably find that such action can earn you $300 to $400 more than the dealer would have offered you and maybe even more than that. If you are buying a very popular new car, the dealer's offer is probably under wholesale for your old one.

The $100 is a flexible figure. You can go up or down as you so desire and the amount of work you put in is also flexible. What you are going to do to this car will include washing, waxing, tire and wheel care, cleaning and spotting the entire interior and trunk, cleaning the engine and the engine compartment, and a tune-up, including oil and filter change and lubrication, replenishment of all the fluids (battery fluid, water coolant, brake fluid, power-steering pump, automatic-transmission fluid, gear lube, rear-end lube, windshield-washer fluid). The idea is to have everything working and sounding right when someone interested in your car steps into it. In most cases, this reconditioning can be done in a single weekend using a combination of your own labor and a professional tune-up shop. Most auto-parts stores will have anything you can possibly need and even tune-up packages if you want to do that yourself.

Detailing When all the basics are done you move in on the fine points. Here is where you become like a professional and do what is known in the car business as "detailing."

1. Lubricate every hinge on the car with the appropriate lubricant. Don't use too much or the lubricant will leak and people will see right away what you have done.
2. Treat all the rubber parts to silicone spray including the door and glass molding and suspension bushings.
3. Get the interior with an application of one of those magic potions—the spot remover or anything that will make it look better.
4. Replace broken knobs, handles, or switches. They are cheap enough, and you will make the car look 100% better.

When you have done all the detailing you can reasonably afford from a time and cash standpoint, take the car out for an hour's drive and listen to it. Make sure everything on the car operates properly. Now you know you have a salable car because you have seen to everything that might detract from its salability. Check the newspaper for prices for your model and put the car up for sale.

Advertise It, Price It, and Say Good-bye

Start off with the tried-and-true method of putting a sign in the car window. This sign will say "For Sale" and will give the price you want and a phone number for a prospective buyer to call. Next, look to the classified ads in the newspaper. Choose a paper with a lot of automobile ads, which generally means that they are effective. People don't put ads where they don't get results. Make up an ad including the year, make, and model, plus a description. Use the exact reading from your odometer for mileage figures from the day you place the ad. List only the most important options—power steering, power brakes (if they are discs say so; those brakes add value), air conditioning, sound system, the transmission type. And if you know the actual factory designation of the color of your car put that in, too. All of this will help sift out the buyers. Don't waste time or money on unimportant options that don't mean anything.

Interested buyers are going to call whatever phone number you put in that ad, so indicate what time they should call or have someone standing by at all times to take a message. People will call back after a busy signal, but they don't call back if the phone just rings and rings.

I believe that you ought to include your asking price in the advertisement. By putting a price in, you haven't really locked yourself in. Most people realize they can dicker and bargain with anyone. What you have done, however, is eliminate the buyer who thinks he or she is going to get a $2,000 car for $200. Stop wasting your time and theirs by putting an approximate price in your ad.

Set the price of your car based on what similar cars are selling for, perhaps adding a little if yours is in excellent condition or more fancily equipped than most, or subtracting a little so you can get a quick sale. In any case, you should know what you think your car is worth. The people answering your ad, though, do not know the value of your car, so you should keep a complete list of options and a basic description beside the phone. Don't oversell it. Say that the only way they will ever know is to come to see you and the vehicle.

Make It Easy on Yourself Set up one evening or one day when you know you will be available and invite as many people as possible to come on that day. Don't let them say, "I will see you tomorrow at 6," or "I'll drop over on Thursday at 7." Whatever. You tell them when you will be available. If you want to space the possible buyers apart, have them come at one-hour intervals. By scheduling in this way, you are not going to be sitting around evening after evening, weekend after weekend, waiting for people who don't show up. If you make four or five appointments within a three- or four-hour period on the weekend, some people will show up, you will be able to show your car, and possibly get your sale.

Decide on the rock bottom price you will accept. Your ad may have stated a price a couple of hundred higher than that. You are willing to dicker, but don't oversell. If you have done the proper work on the car, and the car is a good one, it will sell itself to the right buyer. All you must do is strike a bargain over the price. Don't accept less than your rock bottom, and don't try to skyrocket an extra couple hundred dollars out of the car. Deal on a friendly basis. If you can't deal that way, shake hands, and say good-bye to whoever the customer was.

INDEX